L.L.Bean®

FLY FISHING FOR
STRIPED BASS HANDBOOK

Other L.L. Bean Handbooks

L.L.Bean®

FLY FISHING FOR STRIPED BASS HANDBOOK

BRAD BURNS

Illustrated by John Rice

LYONS PRESS

Printed in Singapore

10 9 8 7 6 5 4 3 2

Design by Desktop Miracles, Dallas, TX

Library of Congress Cataloging-in-Publication Data

Burns, Brad.
    L.L. Bean fly fishing for striped bass handbook / Brad Burns: illustrated by John Rice.
        p. cm.
    Includes index.
    ISBN 1-55821-736-3
    1. Striped bass fishing. 2. Fly fishing. I. Title.
SH691.S7B87   1998
799.1'7732—dc21   98-16674
                                                                              CIP

CONTENTS

ACKNOWLEDGMENTS

Many people were helpful to me in writing this book. I deeply appreciate the warm welcome and candid information that I received from the striped bass fishing fraternity up and down the eastern seaboard. I'm grateful.

Special thanks go first to Joel Yuodsnukis and Jim Rowinski of L.L. Bean. Both men provided me with some great ideas that they will see incorporated in this book. And thanks go to Brock Apfel, who introduced me to the L.L. Bean fly-fishing program some years ago.

Next I'd like to recognize John Rice's brilliant art. Despite the demand for his services, John has donated an original painting to the Coastal Conservation Association every year since it started in the northeast.

John Cole, Duncan Barnes, and George Reiger lent me some of their expertise, enthusiasm, and experience; they are inspirations and friends.

Tom Fote, whose spare bedroom I know well, introduced me to the Jersey Shore. If stripers could walk on land they would build a monument of appreciation to Tom for his conservation efforts on their behalf. The stripers would also get plenty of help from the fluke, weakfish, blues, and tautog.

Tom Earnhardt, Peter Winslow, Dave Rimmer, Harvey Wheeler, Chip Bates, Duncan Barnes, George Reiger, and especially Dick White helped me with slides from their collections to illustrate the upcoming pages. Dick, who I met fishing, also did all of the macro photography.

And finally thanks to George Watson, Pat Abate, Dave Rimmer, and Mark Barnes for their critique of the fishing contents of this book. Hopefully we've added something to this sport and done something for this fish that we all love so much.

Figure 1 *The author (right) and John Cole saw stripers almost disappear—and now revel in their*

FOREWORD

It's a good thing I began fishing with Brad Burns when I did. I was more than 20 years younger then, and I could almost keep up with this single-minded and enthusiastic angler. It's taken me a while to understand just how much of an achievement-oriented man this is. Believe me, you don't meet many folks, fishermen included, with Brad's energy, competitive spirit, and unshakable belief that any and all of life's challenges can be met if he just puts his heart and mind to work.

He called me out of the blue because he'd heard I was a striped bass enthusiast. In Brad's book, anyone with a demonstrable interest in this remarkable creature should be checked out. Thus my first invitation to fish the Kennebec River with Brad aboard his first *Sea Beagle,* then a 24-foot Aquasport. I got an inkling of how seriously he takes his fishing when he said he'd meet me at the local HoJo's at 3:30—that's 3:30 in the morning, some two hours before even the June sun would rise. I'd just gotten to the bacon part of my bacon and eggs when Brad, who had demolished his while I was still unfolding my napkin, said we'd best be going. I looked around at the young people in their party outfits enjoying a snack before they finally headed home to bed and I wondered what I'd gotten myself into.

It was still pitch dark when we let go the mooring and headed downriver. The Kennebec is no lake; it's a twisting, robust river well buttressed with boulders, ledges, and sudden shoals. But Brad stood firm at the *Sea Beagle's* helm as we roared along at close to 20 knots. "Geez," I said to myself, "I sure hope this guy knows what he's doing."

As I've learned many times since, I shouldn't have been the slightest bit concerned. For if ever there was a skipper and an angler—especially a striped bass angler—who knows what he's doing, it's Brad Burns.

On that first dawn, we fished with husky boat rods and star-drag reels, some loaded with wire line, others with 30-pound-test mono: heavy stuff. We trolled

Danny plugs, each the size of a policeman's nightstick, fitted with three sets of treble hooks. A fellow could get tuckered out retrieving just the plug.

Watching for ranges I could only guess at, Brad moved his boat with painstaking precision, lining up for a pass above an invisible lair beneath us where lunker stripers lay like logs in the current. "Get ready," he called. And *pow!*, there was a strike, a thump as solid as if I'd snagged a submerged Buick.

Those huge stripers were there, just where Brad knew they would be. We were hauling in 40- and 50-pounders, and doing it at a time when pretty much everyone was convinced there were no stripers left in the Kennebec, certainly not the trophy fish that came over the *Sea Beagle's* transom—and were gently unhooked and released, by the way. For even then, Brad Burns could not bring himself to kill this creature that he loves so much.

It's been a long march since that first dawn on the Kennebec, that first quite unforgettable meeting with Brad and those humongous stripers. I don't recall precisely when he abandoned boat rods and reels in favor of fly-casting equipment, but of course he did it with his usual single-minded determination and astonishing energy.

Since then we've fished together in Alaska and Iceland, off the Marquesas, off Cape Cod, in the Everglades, along the banks of Maine's Presumpscot River, and, of course, on the Kennebec and each of its sinuous tributaries. Brad has cut a much wider swath. He's been north to Labrador and south to the Chesapeake Bay. I can't keep up with him anymore; I could hardly keep up 20 years ago.

But until I read this book, I never realized just how much there is to keep up with. This man knows more about fly fishing in general—and more about fishing for stripers in particular—than just about anyone I've ever met, or heard about. This is a perfectionist at work here. This is a driven man who wants every aspect of his efforts to be the best there is. The same remarkable energies that powered him away from that HoJo's breakfast table at 3:30 in the morning so that he would be certain to be on the Kennebec well before sunup still drive him toward a single goal—to find and connect with striped bass on a fly.

If you doubt me, read this book. Then you'll know just about everything Brad has learned over all these busy years. And take it from me, this is all you'll ever need to know . . . and then some.

—John Cole

Figure 2 (Photo by Pip Winslow)

STRIPER FISHING

I've stood in the midnight picket line.
Five or six, from all the millions.
At the ocean's edge, and a few feet more,
among our precious fishes.

Rolling, sunlit, foam-edged tide rips, on to the horizon,
or black nights, when an outstretched hand is invisible.
How hard, and tenderly you hold us;
we have learned to love you both.
As May mornings, and southerlies full of summer's promise,
and November afternoons, old, gray, and sullen.

Give us a few more big fish, big smiles,
then let winter's wind come again.
Blow through our open window, across the mugs of coffee,
rustle the flies pinned to the visor, dry the sand we'll find next
    spring.

And we'll sit and talk of nights on the beach,
and dream of being again with our precious fishes.

Fly fishing for stripers is not strictly a phenomenon of modern times. George Reiger's classic work *Profiles in Saltwater Angling* remembers that one of America's first outdoor writers, Henry William Herbert, writing under the pen name of Frank Forester, found the striper to be a handful on salmon-weight fly-fishing equipment, and the finest inshore sea fish of them all. Herbert lived, wrote, and fished from his home on the banks of the then-pristine Passaic River, in mid-19th-century

New Jersey. And doubtless Herbert was not the first to cast a hook decorated with feathers, for stripers. Striped bass fly fishermen would, however, be in a very distinct minority for another hundred years or so: When the fishermen of Herbert's era found the time to go afield, food for the pot was a top priority. And since catches of all fish are easier to make with bait and stiff tackle, that was the method. Possessed of money and time, a few anglers did travel to what are still today's most superb striped bass fishing locations, however. From the comfort of posh clubhouses, fortified with enormous meals, the members fished with the finest equipment of the day, from iron stands built on the boulders of such famous spots as Cuttyhunk, Squibnocket Point, and Montauk. Of course, what is today an affordable drive of a few hours at most was then an overnight trip requiring hired transportation, including boats. These anglers' tackle wasn't usually designed for fly fishing, although by holding onto the rusting pipes of the long-gone Squibnocket bass stand I have pulled myself up on the most seaward boulder and enjoyed some great bass fishing on the fly.

World War II and the graduated income tax changed everything. Men like *Saltwater Sportsman* magazine's Frank Woolner returned from the war to find enough leisure time and automotive technology to range the beaches of Cape Cod, while their counterparts did the same thing from Maine to the Carolina Outer Banks. In their 1954 book, *Striped Bass Fishing,* Frank Woolner and Henry Lyman described the movement to salt water with this sentence: "In 1946, thanks to relative affluence, more rapid transportation, and a burgeoning desire to adventure on earth's last frontier, a vast host of one-time inland anglers swarmed lemminglike to the sea." The fly rod was soon making its way into an occasional photograph. In fact Woolner and Lyman, ahead of their time, did quite a bit of fly fishing for stripers; several pictures of both men with fly rods illustrate the revised version of their book. In the mid- to late 1940s men like Joe Brooks and Nelson Bryant, fishing from opposite sides of America, set world records for striped bass with fish in the high-20-pound range. These were monsters, especially given the tackle that anglers had to work with. I've heard Nelson Bryant, who grew up fishing on Martha's Vineyard, recount the story of his fish—and the "over-40-pounder" he'd lost earlier that same evening. The great bass twice ran Nelson to the very end of the 200 yards of backing on his Pflueger Medalist reel, leaving him barely hanging on and with water trickling over the top of his waders. Finally, in a last roll in the wash, the hook pulled, and Nelson's world record (which would have stood for quite some time) swam wearily out to rejoin the school. Over in Warren, Rhode Island, Harold Gibbs and his brother Frank were designing a pair of striper flies that are tied to this day, and just as effective as ever.

Harold Gibbs took nearly 1,000 bass on the fly in one season in the late 1940s—a very large number even by the standards of today's far-better-equipped angler. The Chesapeake Bay was producing some good year-classes, and the existing commercial-fishing technology, coupled with limited demand, allowed migratory stripers to escape in sufficient numbers to provide a wide diversity of sizes. This included plenty of the large stripers that were then called "bull-bass" and are now more accurately referred to as "cows."

The 1950s and '60s brought about rapid developments in fly-fishing tackle. Fiberglass rods, vinyl-covered lines, mono leaders, and saltwater fly reels with good drags made it easier to cast long distances and fish for longer periods of time. This new tackle also enabled the angler to land more fish, once hooked. Casting techniques like the double haul along with shooting heads and mono running lines made it possible for rising stars like Lefty Kreh to wow the crowds with 100-foot casts. The ability to make a long cast, when needed, is valuable in the search for cow-stripers. And fast-sinking heads with thin running lines make it possible for fly fishermen to compete with conventional-tackle anglers for access to fish lying deep around bottom structure.

By the early 1970s it was clear to anyone whose head wasn't stuck in the sand that the striper was experiencing some bad times. Throughout the late '60s the commercial catch—now called "harvest" in the benign vernacular of fisheries scientists, as if you simply planted baby stripers in the spring—climbed through the roof. Most recreational anglers kept and ate their catch, or gave away all that they caught. The results were all-too-predictable: Stripers slid right off the edge. There were no young stripers along the coast, although the schools of big fish that had escaped the slaughter that befell their brethren kept anglers going. Fisheries managers haggled and dragged their feet until Maryland, faced with the total reproductive failure of the striped bass, closed its side of the Chesapeake to all catching of stripers. To a lesser, but similar, degree, most of the rest of the coast followed. These were the striper's darkest hours. Some states, including Maine, New Hampshire, and New Jersey, put the bad times to some good use by making the striper a personal-use-only species. It was clear to many that even if the striper was to recover, it could never again provide consistent fishing and be managed for maximum sustainable yield (MSY)—a commercial-fishing-management concept that calculates, based on the reproductive capacity of the fish and perceived nonfishing mortality factors, the maximum harvest of stripers from every year-class that can theoretically take place without the collapse of the fishery. Virtually every fish managed under MSY ends up being overfished,

Figure 3   Luckily, these children will be able to enjoy fly fishing for striped bass. (Photo by Chip Bates)

however, since actual mortality from all sources, including unreported commercial harvest, recreational poaching, and commercial by-catch, is difficult to accurately assess. Even the resilient striper, which lives and breeds in the midst of this country's densest human population, can't take this kind of pressure.

In any case the striper did recover, if slowly at first. Small pods of schoolies appeared in the same places that their mothers had first visited 10 or 15 years before. The resurgence of the school stripers was practically a religious experience for those of us who had watched the striper fail. The mid-1980s found measurable annual population increases in striper schools, and the late 1980s began to produce the schools of mixed-size fish that I hadn't seen since my youth. The stripers had come back.

Today, up and down the coast, anglers are discovering striper fishing on the fly rod in greater numbers every year. As the new wave takes hold, people have brought new fly-fishing techniques to the land of stripers. From the South have come flats skiffs with poling platforms, captained around Long Island's Gardiners Bay by shallow-water, sight-fishing guides. On Cape Cod's Monomoy Island a water taxi takes anglers to productive wading flats, then picks them up later in the day. From Europe have come Spey rods with their dedicated following of anglers—who can pick up a sinking head and big fly and, without false casting, hurl it distances that only Superman could achieve with a 9-foot stick. Specially made striper lines, high-tech wading jackets, comfortable mesh vests, reels with excellent drag systems, and about a zillion other enhancements have also come to fly fishing for striped bass. For those of us with some history in stripering, these innovations in techniques and equipment have added new dimensions and efficiency to our quest; far more important, they've greatly enriched our experiences on the water.

There is something else about striper fishing with a fly rod that is unique and close to the heart of L.L. Bean. Fishing for stripers embodies a high-quality, sustainable relationship between man and the out-of-doors. Healthy for both the body and soul and with limited impact on the resource, fly fishing for stripers is developing a large and devoted following. Adding to this is another great thing about the striper: the kind of place it calls home. Over 20 million East Coast residents can leave their urban jobs at 5:30 and, with but a half hour's after-dinner drive, walk into the water or launch their tin boat into the still-wild ocean and fish for stripers. According to the United States Fish and Wildlife Service, over 1.7 million did just that in 1996, and this number is growing every year. This is the kind of recreational opportunity that makes sense today. These are wild fish, the survivors of pollution, overfishing, and the many other effects of urbanization—and they still grow to 40 or 50 pounds, they still swallow whole 2-pound bunkers, and an encounter with them is available to anyone who will diligently cast a fly into the Atlantic. Look out from any of a thousand spits of East Coast shorefront to the often-empty surface of the sea and you could almost be on this planet alone, despite a city of a million or more that would be clearly visible if you just turned around. What's more, the striper season starts up in March south of New Jersey, and ends up in December in North Carolina. The striper's vast migration up and down the populous East Coast lends itself to satisfying the wanderlust of even the most fanatical fishermen. If you were so inclined, you could chase the striper from snow season to snow season, fishing every weekend from somewhere between Maine and North Carolina, and even fishing the warm power-plant outflows when the rest of the world is frozen stiff.

This book is to help you enjoy the world of the striped bass as a fly fisher, which is as close as you can come to meeting the bass on its own terms. In a while I'll discuss in some depth the creature itself—its physical design, food preferences, feeding habits, preferred environments, and migratory timetables. I'll also discuss fly tackle, clothing, gear, boats, and many other things that can help you not only catch stripers but thoroughly enjoy the experience as well. Perhaps you will one day decide, as I have, that the striper is the ultimate inshore, saltwater fly-rod gamefish.

PART I

The Fish and Its Forage

Figure 4   The striped bass, front and side views.

CHAPTER 1

Biology and Observation

It's a good idea to know as much about your quarry as possible. Not only will this help you catch more fish, but you'll also simply enjoy knowing a little bit about what it is that makes the striper tick. I'll start with the physical design of the striped bass, so you can understand how it might hunt its prey (Fig. 4).

The striper has an elongated body that is moderately compressed from side to side. This characteristic means that the striper is not only a fairly fast swimmer, but also an agile one. By using its body height, the fish can turn quickly in the water. A glance at the drawing of the striper also reveals its large, clearly developed fins. Fins are like rudders in the water; having such large fins makes the striper highly maneuverable, hence its reputation for being at home in turbulent environments. The tail of the striped bass is tall, nearly square, and thickly joined to the body, eliminating the need for the supporting keels found on tuna, but sacrificing their streamlined design. This tail is designed for short-burst power, not high-speed ocean swimming. The striper also has a clearly visible, highly developed **lateral line**. This line possesses sensors that allow the bass to feel the vibrations of its prey, or the approach of predators. If you couple the lateral line with the striper's large and prominent eye, you have a night feeder, a fish at ease in low-light conditions. The striper's namesake is its six or seven stripes, which combine with a dark back and silvery sides used to break up light. This camouflage design is made to hide the striper against the bottom, and to use sunlight to break up its image in shallow water. Finally, the striper has a large mouth that gapes back to its eye and is filled with small, pointed teeth, which also cover its tongue. These are not long teeth made to cut; they feel more like a rasp, and are designed to hold slippery food so that it can be crushed and then swallowed. Under the skin of its body the striper has thickly muscled sides that are largely made up of white muscle, as you might find in a groundfish like a cod. But these muscles are also heavily interspersed with dark reddish tissue, as you might find in a tuna or bluefish. These two types of muscle serve different purposes: The white muscle provides quick energy for short bursts (again, you might expect this from a predatory groundfish like a cod or haddock). The dark muscles, on the other hand, can retain oxygen for swimming at sustained higher speeds, but once exhausted they require a longer recovery time. Stripers need their dark muscles for surface feeding and for the extensive swimming required by their 1,000-mile migrations.

How about the mind of the bass? How much of our strategy is this fish capable of unraveling? Some years ago a group of us were holed up on Block Island during a November snowstorm. The conversation about—what else?—the wily striped bass was broken up by a hoot from Fred Thurber, who was pawing through one of the back-to-nature books that he was always reading. "Look at this," said Fred, suddenly quite serious. In order to illustrate the evolution of the simplest brain and central nervous system, a diagram of a fish, pointing out its pea-size brain, was captioned MORONE SAX-ATILIS, THE STRIPED BASS. We were certain that it was a misprint; how could our noble quarry be equipped with only the bare minimum for a brain? It was, of course, accurate, and using this information to plan my tactics has added to my success at catching stripers. Fish, including stripers, act out of instinct and to fill basic needs. They aren't afraid of hooks, since they have no idea what a hook is. They also aren't leader-shy, since they have no concept of a leader. A fly, however, may not seem like food to the striper if it has no action because the leader is too heavy or is knotted rigidly to the fly. When a striper follows its hooked companion to the boat, it's not out of sympathy—it's to steal the food hanging out of the hooked fish's mouth. When you try to anticipate bass behavior in order to tie a fly, pick a place to fish, or land a strong fighter, think in terms of the emotionless survival instincts that rule life as a wild fish. Leave out the complicated emotions and rationalizations that characterize human thinking.

You can understand a lot about the striped bass from these physical and mental descriptions. Let me now use this new insight to further your understanding of the striper by designing a feeding station, then studying the way the striper uses it to attack its prey.

Just after daybreak the tide starts to flow out of a coastal river. Herring, feeding on plankton in the brackish water, drift downstream rather than fight the oncoming current. In a back eddy formed by a finger of ledge jutting off a point that extends into the river, the bass can rest easily, using their large fins and broad tails to effortlessly hold their positions. Meanwhile, with their lateral lines and large eyes they survey the shallow, dark water rushing over the top of the ledge. Too late, in the dim morning light, the school of herring sees the bass; swimming with difficulty in the turbulent water, the panicked herring rush to the surface to escape. The bass leap from their resting places behind the rocks, propelled to full speed in an instant by quick thrusts of their broomlike tails. Like landing nets with built-in vacuum pumps, the bass's big mouths are deployed, sucking in water and herring; the latter are held from escape in the one-way grip of hundreds of sharp teeth that point toward the

Figure 5   Look at the powerful shoulders and tail of this prime bass. Is there a more beautiful example of a fish? (Photo by Chip Bates)

striper's crusher plates. Quickly the herring are squeezed lifeless by these plates in the backs of the bass's throats, then swallowed. With a thrust of their powerful tails and a little steerage from their pectoral and dorsal fins, the bass are back on station.

The striped bass is perfectly adapted for its role as the top predator in its inshore environment. In the next chapter I will cover, in diagram and text, how to identify and effectively fish structure like the one I just described, along with other likely feeding habitats for striped bass.

Some of the rest of the striper's biology is less directly important to catching stripers, but still of great interest to anglers. When I talk about stripers, I'm frequently asked questions like: How big do they get? When do the first ones show up in the spring? Are the fish in New England males or females? Let me thus review for you the fascinating behavior of the migrating stripers and add some more helpful information about the creature's biology.

CHAPTER 2

The Migration

The more I read and hear about it, the more complex and unpredictable I find the striped bass migration to be. While we have a basic idea of what migrating stripers do, my friend Kenny Vanderlaske has a good point: "How can we know? They're under water, they've got fins, they go where they want." We do know, however, that virtually all stripers spawn south of New England, swim north in the spring, and return south in the fall. And without question the major spawning area for striped bass is the Chesapeake Bay. The Hudson River is also important, but is a very distant number two. Delaware Bay has a population, too, which has come back from near-extinction caused by industrial pollution along its thickly settled banks. The size of its contribution is unknown, but thought to be relatively minor. Several of the Carolina sounds send stripers out to the coast; one, the Roanoke, was once a big producer. Back in the 1950s and '60s, when male and female stripers rose to the surface of the Roanoke to spawn, the vogue was for boats to speed over to the commotion and scoop up all the spawning bass in a monstrous net. This brought on the inevitable: The fishery nearly became extinct. Now the population is at least stable, if no longer a big component of the East Coast stock. Up where I live, in Maine, striped bass once again spawn in the Kennebec River, but their population is thought to be still quite small. Given the recent discovery of inch-long stripers in the Connecticut

River, it appears that some bass spawn there as well, but this hasn't been formally verified. There are South Atlantic bight and Canadian populations, too, but these are small, localized, and outside the scope of this book.

Striped bass are **anadramous** fish, spawning in the spring in fresh water, then returning to salt or brackish water to live. (**Pelagic** fish are ocean spawning.) Their requirements for spawning and nursery areas are very specific. Spawning takes place in April and May in the Chesapeake Bay and its tributaries; late May in the Hudson; and late May or June in the Kennebec.

Females start becoming sexually mature at five years old, and most are fully mature by their eighth or ninth year; males start maturing at three years of age. A female is often attended by a number of males that excitedly push the eggs from her sides, then squirt them with milt. Males can spawn several times in the course of one spawning season; females, only once. Big cow-bass hold millions of eggs and are valuable to the population for both their gene pool and their fecundity.

Newly hatched stripers drift freely with the current for a day or two, then, after consuming their yolk sac, start their new lives as predators. They live in fresh or brackish estuaries until they are at least two years old, at which point they are between 9 and 11 inches long. In the spring of their third year of life, a small percentage of females join older bass that have wintered in the bays or along the coast and migrate northward, presumably because the bays cannot supply enough food to feed all of the adult stripers that have their roots in one particular spawning area. The following year this percentage of migrators is much larger—it increases from around 20 percent to around 75 percent, at least according to some studies. Most of the male population and a few of the females are thought to remain near their spawning grounds their entire lives.

The migration of three-year-olds is the reason you will commonly see a lot of 16-inch bass along the New England shore in the spring, and so many 18- or 19-inchers heading back south in the fall. See how well we feed them? They grow 3 inches in four months! Indeed, stripers can grow very large, and individuals have been documented that weighed over 100 pounds. In a population with a natural year-class distribution (one in which overfishing hasn't taken too many fish from a particular year-class), stripers of 40 to 50 pounds are common enough to be found in schools. Conservation-minded anglers should realize that almost all coastal stripers are females, the breeders of the present and the future.

The fall southward migration is an even more complex phenomenon. Not all the fish migrate all the way south, for one thing; also, as in the spring, they certainly don't all do it at the same time. In recent years of small-striper abundance, mass over-wintering has been observed at places like Scorton Creek, on Cape Cod (where some are killed by the winter cold), and the Thames River in Connecticut, where an over-winter fishery occurs every year (the heart of it lying between the Interstate 95 over-pass and downtown Norwich). The bulk of the striper population winters over either in the Hudson River, in the deep channels of the Chesapeake Bay, or along the beaches from New Jersey down to the Carolina capes, where fish are caught sporadi-cally during the winter. Perhaps the strangest wintering-over story ever told is of a striper tagged by Canadian officials in March, presumably as part of a small popula-tion that exists in the Kouchibouguac River in New Brunswick. The 24-inch fish was recaptured in Maryland less than two weeks later after a 1,500-mile swim through a winter sea to reach her spawning grounds! She had probably also migrated this far north—considering her youth—the previous spring. Despite the vagaries of the migratory patterns, here's a general timetable for spring and fall migrations.

First Dependable Spring Fishing

The Carolina Sounds and Chesapeake Bay

Stripers winter here and warm days can produce fish in the channels; activity starts in earnest by the end of March or early April. Large fish move toward the spawning areas in March and are available until late May or early June, when most of them move out to the coast.

Delaware Bay and the Hudson River

These spawning areas are similar to the Chesapeake, but activity starts a couple of weeks later. The large flats in the Hudson, near the Tappan Zee Bridge, start to warm in late March. Prime spawning time, and the greatest availability of big stripers, is during May and early June; then they migrate out to the coast.

The Oceanfront Delmarva Peninsula, New Jersey Shoreline, Southern New York, Long Island Shoreline, and Western Long Island Sound

Starting in late March off the Virginia capes, and progressing to New York by early to late April, the ocean migration of small stripers moves northward very quickly. Large females are available about two weeks to a month later.

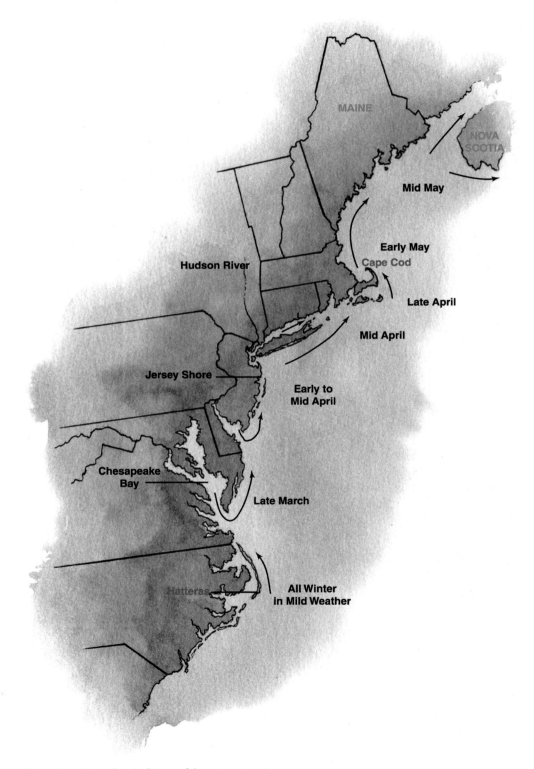

Figure 6a   Normal arrival times of the spring migration.

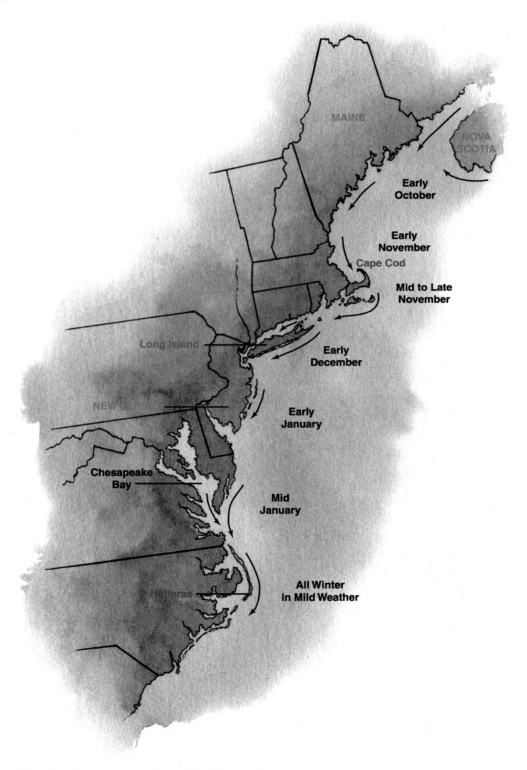

MAINE

NOVA SCOTIA

Early October

Early November

Cape Cod

Mid to Late November

Long Island

Early December

NEW JERSEY

Early January

Chesapeake Bay

Mid January

Hatteras

All Winter in Mild Weather

Figure 6b   Normal departure times of the fall migration.

Eastern New York to Southern Cape Cod

Schoolies start appearing in New York in mid-April; late April on Cape Cod. Larger fish arrive about one month later.

Cape Cod Bay to Maine

Schoolies arrive in late April in Cape Cod Bay, and in mid-May in Maine's Kennebec River. Larger fish show up in late May near the Cape Cod Canal and reach the Kennebec around mid-June.

I find the fall migration a bit more confusing and unpredictable than the spring, but I can offer you no really good reason why this should be. Interestingly, stripers leave most places with water warmer than 50 degrees during the fall, but they arrive during the spring to water that is considerably cooler. Stripers arrive in Maine within 30 days of the longest day of the year, yet they don't leave until 90 days after the summer solstice. So it is unclear exactly which combination of these two factors—water temperature and day length—or others triggers the migratory movement. I'm certainly glad that the fish have a few secrets. Here's my crack at the fall southward migration timetable.

Last Striper Trip of the Fall

Maine

Most bass are gone from Maine by October 1.

Cape Ann to the Canal

While striper action in this area seems to get going all at once in the spring, the fall is more complicated. The Plum Island area really thins out by mid-October; add two or three weeks for Boston's South Shore. The Brewster flats on the Cape and anywhere in the canal can produce into November. The great beaches off Cape Cod peak in mid-October and are done by the first of November.

Cape Cod's South Shore to Montauk

I can usually find bass near Woods Hole into the second week of November. Block Island fishing continues to late November, and Montauk into early December.

Everywhere South of Long Island Sound

Stripers routinely winter over in the Hudson and all along the beaches from New Jersey to Cape Hatteras. Fish often hold in all of these areas into mid- or late December before becoming dormant for the winter. The season may last a week or two longer off the Chesapeake Bay Bridge Tunnel than in New York Harbor, but this isn't certain. In recent years several magazines have published stories on Christmas striper fishing in New York Harbor. Fishermen throughout this stretch usually give up before the fish do. Not that they're wimps—fly fishing is tough in 30-degree weather.

Perhaps the most important lesson for East Coasters in all of this information is that, first, by late April you can start fishing for stripers somewhere within a few hours' drive. And if you're willing to make a maximum drive of five hours for a weekend's fishing, you don't have to give up until at least Thanksgiving. Clean a few lines, tie a few flies, make a little peace with your spouse (skip this if you're one of the growing number of fly-fishing couples), and in the time it takes to schedule a dental checkup you can be back fishing for stripers.

CHAPTER 3

Forage Fish

I once read a report on a population of striped bass that lived in a Canadian estuary on the Northumberland shore. Examining the stomach contents of the bass revealed to Canadian fisheries scientists that these stripers ate virtually every living creature that resided with them in the river. This incredible versatility as feeders, of course, requires that the fish be equally versatile as hunters. And it is this versatility that makes the striper such a superb fly-rod target. I've often said that if I had just one species to pursue, I'd want it to be the striper, which acts like several fish wrapped into one. Last spring, for example, I was fishing on Cape Cod from my base on Falmouth's shore. I could fish the Vineyard Sound tide rips, the riverlike currents of the holes in the Elizabeth Islands, and the salt ponds of the Cape's south shore. In the rips the bass were pounding on the spring squid run; in the holes they were cornering herring and bunker; and in the ponds the stripers ate marine worms, mummichogs, and spearing. To imitate these baitfish required everything from a 12-weight rod with a 550-grain head to a 4-weight outfit, floating line, and tiny flies.

Sometimes stripers are opportunistic and will hit anything that moves near them. At other times they can be very selective, especially as to the size and action of the bait. This can be confusing when you're selecting a fly or determining the cadence of its retrieve. While fishing, I often wonder if a change of retrieve or fly pattern would be productive, while at the same time being hesitant to invest extra time in a seemingly unproductive piece of water. Luckily for the striper fisherman, if feeding bass are present in enough numbers to warrant the time it takes to change flies or lines, or simply to make repeat drifts over a structure, something will give the presence of those fish away. For example, toss a fly into a current seam at a tidal creek outflow; if there are bass present, they're likely to at least boil under it, or follow behind it. When stripers are feeding on the surface or in shallow water, their presence is detectable by the splashes or swirls that they make. Even at night, the feeding pops and splashes of hungry bass can be heard from some distance. Their surface swirls along a shallow beach are often clearly visible. Once you have located feeding stripers, you can settle into imitating whatever bait they're chasing. As with the bass themselves, a little knowledge of the primary striper baitfish can help you judge the likelihood that any particular baitfish will be present where you're fishing, and what types of fly and retrieve are most likely to score. In the rest of this chapter I will list and discuss each major striper food fish. I'll also suggest flies to emulate these fish, as well as telling you how to tie several of the most important and versatile of these patterns.

Herring

Everything that I have read on striped bass, as well as my own experience, has told me that the striper's preferred food is soft-rayed finfish. Along the striper coast,

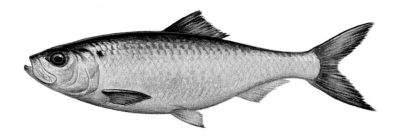

Figure 7   Blueback herring.

herring—both mature and immature, anadramous and pelagic—are one of the most important prey species for stripers. The design of the herring family makes them perfect food for bass. Herring are more catchable than a rapid swimmer like a mackerel;

swim in very large schools, which provide food for whole schools of bass; and have soft fins and bodies for ease of swallowing. Their fat, oily bodies are highly nutritious, since they possess five times the caloric count of a lean fish like a cod. There are herring of various sizes and species available throughout the striper's migration up and down the East Coast from Maine to North Carolina.

Two species of herring—**alewives,** nicknamed buckies, and a close relative, the **blueback herring**—are both anadramous species. These species run up the coastal brooks and rivers in the spring in order to spawn. Their young swim back down to the sea from late summer into early winter. **Atlantic herring** (pelagic) spawn all along the shores of New England throughout the year, with the possible exception of the dead of winter. Once born, the tiny herring make their way to inshore waters, where they are nourished on the rich life available there. The adult Atlantic herring themselves come into coastal waters and estuaries to feed. The overall patterns of all these various sizes, types, and ages of herring defies simple description, and it is not necessary to try. The important thing to know is that stripers, at virtually any time or place in their migration, may be feeding on herring in sizes from 1 inch to 1½ feet. Look for alewives and blueback herring to be heading up rivers in the late spring and early summer, often joined in lower rivers by full-size Atlantic herring. You may also find small Atlantic herring in rivers and along beachfronts throughout the season, but especially in the early summer. Look for young alewives in the early fall as the young drop back to the sea. Herring are not necessarily obvious, even when present in great numbers. You may sometimes snag them on your fly, if they are thick; or you may see stripers chase herring to the surface, where they may be caught by birds. And you may find dead herring along a shoreline, indicating that stripers are feeding on them just offshore. Occasionally, on very still mornings, herring can be seen finning on the surface. Sometimes the location of stripers feeding on herring below the surface will be given away by a "slick" or calm area on the water, caused by oil released from the crushed and mangled bodies of these baitfish.

Herring of all species, including **shad** (a type of anadramous herring that can grow to 6 pounds or larger), have long and slender bodies and are very compressed from side to side. They also have rainbow-colored sides, often with a pink hue, and blue and/or greenish backs, with white bellies.

When it comes to flies that imitate herring—or for that matter many of the other bite-size finfish available to stripers—the selection is mind boggling. I feel that having all or most of these patterns involves unnecessary duplication, but they may be fun to tie anyway. Frank Daignault, who has written prolifically about stripers, once said in a magazine piece that no one had proved to him that anything worked better for stripers than a few pieces of saddle hackle wrapped onto a hook. Frank frequently fishes at night on the outer Cape beaches, and given that environment especially, I think his view has a lot of wisdom. Herring and all finfish wiggle very much like wet feathers. Since I do a lot of daylight fishing, I believe in having a fly look as realistic as possible; and because I like to make use of every advantage, I carry a more complicated assortment of flies for my fishing. I do believe, however, that many anglers are far too concerned with pattern, and often end up with flies that catch more fishermen than they do fish. Many of today's flashy patterns are delicate or hard bodied, of poor proportion, or tied with stiff materials that neither breathe nor wiggle in the water. Entire books, some of them quite good, have been written on baitfish and flies to imitate them. I find these books informative and, as a fly tyer, inspirational; however, I think you will be better served by the short list of versatile flies that I will present in chapter 6.

As a general rule, flies intended to duplicate full-size herring should have considerable flash material along their sides, wiggle easily in the water, and have obvious eyes. They should be sufficiently bulky to push enough water aside to imitate a foot-long fish in panicked flight, be moderately tall for their length, but be thin from side to side. You should have a selection in white with green or blue tops, since these are the natural herring colors. You should also have some in yellow or chartreuse if you will be fishing in silty waters like river systems; and in black, to silhouette against the sky, for low-light or nighttime conditions.

Herring and menhaden (see below) are robust swimmers. Baitfish like these are worth a great effort to a striper. To achieve realism, I often retrieve with long, rapid strips, to imitate a large baitfish in panicked flight. Bass may very well be excited into striking by seeing a big fly that they believe is a herring about to escape. The former director of L.L. Bean's fly-fishing school, Brock Apfel, introduced me to super-aggressive stripping some years ago. He caught three fish to my one until I caught on.

Menhaden (Bunker, Mossbunker, Pogies)

Menhaden swim north in the springtime from their overwintering areas along the mid-Atlantic. Spawning takes place all along the route from spring through fall. A big difference between herring and menhaden is that while herring of all sizes are present throughout the striper's range, small menhaden (young-of-the-year) are present only from July, at locations south of New England, to the late summer and

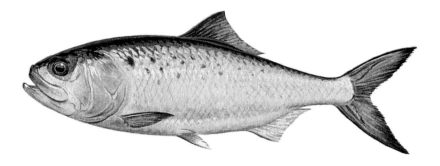

Figure 8   Menhaden.

fall in southern New England. I have seen large bunker in Maine's Kennebec River as late as mid-October and as early as mid-June. Thus, they are available throughout the migration period of all stripers large enough to eat them. Menhaden are not anadramous; they spawn at sea, and are seldom found far from salt water. Members of the herring family, these fish are tall, and thin from side to side for their length; their flesh and fins are very soft and oily. Menhaden are, however, thicker and more robust than herring. They're bluish gray on the back with silvery rose-tinted sides and a whitish belly. Menhaden also have one or more dark spots on their sides that may serve as false eyes to confuse their many predators.

As fish food, bunker are among the best, and when they are available I have seen bass forsake even herring to chase them exclusively . This is especially true of larger bass. Bunker are often obvious when they're in your area since they travel in large schools and splash on the surface of the water, even when they're not being chased. Young bunker do the same thing but on a much smaller scale; sometimes they look like a patch of disturbed or nervous water. It is not unusual for bunker and herring to travel together. I have netted them both at the same time in a 50-foot length of gill net.

Flies for bunker are essentially interchangeable with herring flies, and I would simply echo my comments on

Figure 9   A big fly, but an even bigger baitfish. (Photo by Pip Winslow)

flies for herring—with one exception: While the maximum length of both fish is similar, menhaden are stockier and higher from belly to back than herring of the same length. To imitate this larger fish I tie my herring flies extra high in the back for height, with more material in the sides for thickness and synthetics that stretch beyond the tail feathers for more length.

Spearing (Silversides, Sperling)

Figure 10   Silverside (spearing).

Spearing are common in estuaries from the Chesapeake Bay to Labrador. It is easy to identify them—a very prominent silver line runs the length of their sides. The backs of silversides are green, the belly white, and they are quite thin, almost tubular, in their body shape. Large adult spearing are only about 5 inches long, with the average being 2 to 3 inches.

Spearing are near-shore creatures that spawn in the salt bays or brackish estuaries along our shorelines. Spawning takes place in the spring, and while young spearing are undoubtedly consumed by other fish, there is no need to present flies to exclusively imitate anything smaller than 2 or 3 inches. This is because all sizes are normally present at once in the same general area, so if smaller spearing are available, it's almost certain that larger ones will, too.

While not found in huge oceangoing schools like menhaden, silversides are nonetheless an important staple of many inshore predators, especially the striper. Hard to see during the day, they typically sink to the bottom, where their small bodies and dark backs leave them quite inconspicuous. At night, however, spearing move close to the shore and hide in the surface film. Shining a flashlight on the surface of a fall salt pond will often cause spearing to jump all over its surface. When you extinguish the light, the fish will simply lie motionless in the surface film. The same is true along a surf line or inside a rocky bowl. I assume this to be a predator-avoidance technique. If you're fishing at night in areas of slow-moving, shallow water that contain spearing, it's a good idea to have some floating flies in your bag. You can often hear the sucking sounds and pops made by the tails of bass taking spearing from the surface. Retrieve your fly by making a slight twitch, and then **dead drift** (making no retrieve at all, but simply allowing it to drift in the current) it for 15 or 20 seconds before your next twitch. This approach can work when nothing else will touch a fish. Despite their small size, spearing can produce big fish for you. In 1994 Ken and Lori Vanderlaske discovered a school of 30- to 40-plus-inch bass moving at dusk onto a Martha's Vineyard beach that were feeding exclusively on spearing. Only a dead-drifted fly would get hits from these selective fish. I arrived on the third night and took a 38-inch striper on a 2-inch Farnsworth floating fly after allowing it to dead drift for about 30 seconds. The strike was so soft that it didn't seem like the bass really meant it. She just sucked it in; bass of this size feeding on such small bait don't waste a lot of energy.

Mullet

Mullet are present from the Deep South to the south side of Cape Cod. In August of both 1996 and 1997, I found stripers and bluefish regularly feeding on

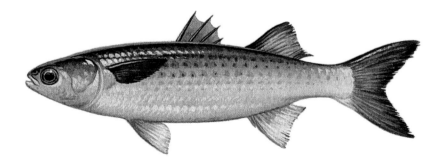

Figure 11   Mullet.

mullet in the Elizabeth Islands. In the North, these are midsummer fish that generally reach a maximum of 6 to 8 inches in length, but they get much larger in the South. Few striped bass anglers talk much about mullet, except during the fall "mullet run." Within the striper's range, mullet don't seem to be a dominant prey species like other large oily fish—herring and menhaden. From North Carolina to Maine I found no one who thought it necessary to imitate juvenile mullet.

A moderate-size Groceries fly tied with a blue-and-green back seems to work well in the Elizabeths when mullet are present. I'm confident that a smaller Deceiver would also work well on young-of-the-year sizes.

Squid

Squid are such an important food of striped bass that historically stripers were nicknamed squidhounds. In the past, when squid populations were greater, stripers were known to chase them into windrows on the beach. How would you like to have

Figure 12   Squid.

been there with your 10-weight while 4-foot stripers chased squid from the water onto the sand at your feet? Squid migrate inshore in the spring, from south to north up the coast. In my southern Cape Cod stomping grounds, squid arrive as soon as the bass, in late April or early May, and they're still around in some numbers well into November. Squid are shy and retreating during the day, but they can be very aggressive at night. My first experiences with squid were 20 years ago on Martha's Vineyard. We caught them from the docks at night using small white jigs, then used them as bait for bottom fishing for stripers. I'll bet that two-thirds of the Vineyard Derby winners of the last 40 years have been caught on squid. Squid are available from the beach out to the farthest offshore locations frequented by stripers. With sizes ranging from slightly over a foot in length down to tiny young-of-the-year (I've seen these being eaten in Long Island Sound in October), squid are second only to herring in importance as striper food.

Squid uniquely propel themselves through the water by sucking water into their flexible body, or **mantle,** and then blowing it out rapidly in a jet stream. This stream is powerful enough to shoot them well out of the water. Still, you'd be lucky to see bass chasing squid to the surface these days; your most likely proof of their presence would be to see bass disgorge them during or after a fight, or to have a squid actually take your fly. (This has happened to me on several occasions—watch out for ink.)

Squid-imitating flies for stripers should be retrieved so that they pulse quickly through the water, and then coast. A long strip can accomplish this quite well. In their relaxed state squid are transparent to almost white in color, but when excited they can turn red or purple. Some very fancy squid patterns are available, including those with mantles constructed of silicone. A big white Deceiver, perhaps with a pink or red feather on each side, will do the job as well as anything.

Sand Eels (Sand Launces, Sand Lances)

Figure 13   Sand eel.

Sand eels are another fish that, conveniently for the striper, are found from North Carolina to beyond Maine. Bigelow and Schroeder's *Fishes of the Gulf of Maine* says that "the slender, round-bodied sand launces suggest small eels in general appearances. Eel-like, too, they lack ventral fins, and they swim with eel-like undulations from side to side. But they are not even remote relatives of the true eels." Sand eels are about 10 times as long as they are tall, and essentially tubular in design. The colors of the sand eel change quickly upon death to a steel blue back, gray sides, and whitish belly. In life, however, they have the iridescent, rainbow-colored sides noted on so many of the shallow-water fish that are the stripers' prey. Like herring and bunker, sand eels are oily fish with a high caloric content; they're probably tasty to stripers as well as nutritious.

Sand eels are found in areas with sandy bottoms, where they use their sharp snouts to burrow 4 to 6 inches into the sand to hide during the day. At night, or during the day in deeper water, they come out to eat. Stripers are often seen feeding on sand eels over large patches of shallow sandy bottom, their tails waving in the air as they root hoglike in the sand to chase out the sand eels.

Flies to imitate sand eels should be very supple, long, thin, and tubular, with shiny sides. This is the bait that Frank Daignault so commonly encountered on the outer Cape Cod beaches and imitated with a few saddle hackles on a hook—which I agree is probably as effective a fly as anything. But like a true tackle addict, I usually can't bear to fish with flies quite that simple, and I often add heads with eyes, and long lengths of thin flash material. Most of the fishing that I do when sand eels are the likely prey, I do by wading. Because of this I use a stripping basket (see pages 87 and 88) and, therefore, a two-handed retrieve. One easy variation of the two-handed retrieve is to move only your hands and wrists as they rest on the edges of your basket. This movement produces a slow, side-to-side, wagging kind of retrieve that works well when sand eels are the dominant bait in the area. Most sand eel flies should be from 4 to 6 inches long. Black is a good nighttime color; white is better by day. I often tie sand eel patterns for beach fishing that include both of these colors. Thin-tied Deceivers, Clousers, or fur-strip flies all make excellent sand eel imitations. The color of the top of the fly may be important with sand eel imitations, because this is one of the few baitfish that the striper often attacks from above.

In case you think that cow-stripers won't eat a little bait like the sand eel, you should know that sand eels are also a favorite food of fin whales.

Grass Shrimp

Fishing the coastal rivers of Maine as an adolescent, I frequently cleaned the small stripers that I sold around the neighborhood. And grass shrimp were present in the stomach of virtually every fish I cleaned. I don't know if these are a preferred food or simply one that is available. The coastal marshes all along the eastern seaboard are home to vast numbers of grass shrimp; they move into slightly deeper water for the winter, but are inshore during the entire striper migration. Grass shrimp are small, usually around an inch in length, but their antennae, tail, and legs give them a larger presence in the water.

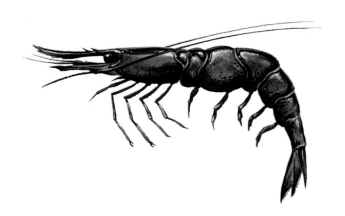

Figure 14   Grass shrimp.

I have tied numerous flies in the past that looked very much (at least to me) like grass shrimp. My luck with these flies, however, has been no better than with small Deceivers or fur-strip patterns tied in white, olive, or black for night fishing. While shrimp normally move slowly forward through the water, indicating a slow retrieve, when they're scared (as they certainly must be when chased by a striped bass) they jet away with rapid beats of the tail. I sometimes retrieve grass shrimp flies with short, quick strips to imitate this action. Grass shrimp are often the target of nighttime feeding in quiet waters—look for boils near the surface, but not loud splashy breaks.

Marine Worms

There are at least a half-dozen prominent species of marine worms throughout the striper's range. Some of them can be well over a foot long, like the sandworms and bloodworms—both armed with teeth—that, as a boy, I fished live from the

Figure 15   Sandworm (clam worm).

bridges along Maine's coastal rivers. Some species, like the cinder worms found in Long Island Sound and south, are very thin and tiny. Unless you are experiencing a worm hatch, or **swarm,** you probably won't see many worms, and the stripers present will only forage on them opportunistically, not as primary feeding targets. Thus you only need accurate facsimiles of worms when they are swarming in their spawning ritual.

Swarming takes place in shallow bays or near mud flats, where the worms live. The most likely time for a swarm is during the dark of the moon in late spring or early summer. Some swarms have become famous; local experts can look at next year's calendar and predict the nights they're most likely to take place. When you encounter a swarm of spawning worms in good striper country, you will know. The worms are weak swimmers and are present from the top to the bottom of the water column. Bass take them the way trout take nymphs, leaving surface and subsurface boils as they feed. Still, duplicating what bass see in these worms is sometimes maddening. For me the most supple, wriggly, authentic-looking patterns have sometimes—but not always—been successful. I've had my best luck fishing in swarms with a floating line and a small (1 to 2 inches tied on a #2 hook) dark-colored Clouser Minnow. Because the swarming worms rise and fall aimlessly, changing directions as they mill about, retrieve with short, moderately slow, sporadic strips of the Clouser, which will do its own bobbing up and down as you retrieve it. I find that black or olive works best, even though the worms appear red in the water; interestingly, the worm's color changes to olive green when it's taken out of the water. If you don't have a fly of the correct length, try modifying one to the length you need in the field with a pair of nippers.

Bay Anchovies

Figure 16   Bay anchovy.

The northern end of the bay anchovy's abundant range is the area from Montauk over to the Rhode Island shoreline. These anchovies, along with their larger cousins the **striped anchovies,** are small, oily, inshore fish whose range extends considerably southward from that of the striper. Unlike spearing—the other important small baitfish of this type—bay anchovies can be found near or at the surface in densely packed schools, which in the fall are visible near shore as amoeboid, undulating brown areas in the water.

The bay anchovy, which seldom grows to over 2 inches in length, is brown on top with a silver line along its side. It looks much like a spearing, but is smaller and has a bright silver patch on its chest. All the major inshore predators, including the striper, love this baitfish. As the gamefish encircle the schools, the surface seems to boil with their nervous movements; then the predators rocket through the anchovy ranks, only to disappear and let the school re-form. I once saw in Montauk a school of bass so engrossed in feeding on bay anchovies, and bay anchovies so engrossed in trying to escape, that when a wave receded from a large flat rock upon which a surf caster was perched it left a layer of slithering anchovies, along with a few flopping stripers, high and dry for a few seconds—all at the feet of the excited fisherman.

There is little point in blind casting with a search pattern as small as a bay anchovy. The time to cast tiny flies of this type is when you see bass actually feeding on a particular bait. Fortunately, it's not hard to recognize bass blitzing bay anchovies. There are several good patterns to imitate this bait, but as I have seen on many occasions, it is the size and profile that you must duplicate. In many cases, especially during a blitz, allow your offering to sink slowly, like a stunned baitfish, and dead drift it as close to the center of the mayhem as you can put it. I like a fly called the Juve, which I will detail on page 72, or a thinly tied Bob Popovics invention called the 3-D, which is simply alternating layers of FisHair and Lite Brite, trimmed into shape. Have both 1- and 2-inch sizes to match the size of the anchovies present. Last fall, while fishing for false albacore in the Fishers Island Race, I was going begging with normally productive patterns, until the one foolish fish that I caught spit up a handful of ³/₄-inch-long anchovies. With my line clippers, I shortened and thinned the 3-D on my line and started catching fish regularly.

Crabs

I struggled over whether I should include crabs under "Other Baitfish" or give them a separate category as an important bait to fly fishermen. What settled my decision were the facts that bass definitely eat crabs, that many traditional baits have been commercially overfished, and that flats fishing has become so popular of late. Common crabs along the striper coast are the **green crab, blue crab, fiddler crab,** and, in the northern ranges, **jonah** or **rock crab**—although keep in mind that there are other species as well.

Figure 17a   Green crab.

Crabs don't swim near enough to the surface of the water to provide much visual evidence that stripers are eating them. This is less troublesome than it sounds, however. For one thing, if you drift over a flat that holds bass and see crabs crawling along, or find them spit up by a caught fish, you will know that crabs are the likely forage. Also, I believe that some simple techniques will give you a shot at catching stripers if crabs are the bait. First, with the exception of blue crabs—which are good swimmers—crabs hug the bottom, so your fly needs to be on the

Figure 17b   Blue crab.

bottom to imitate a crab. The place where you make a presentation must thus be suitable for crab life, and clean enough so you don't hang up on every cast. Many times this means a sand or mud flat clear of most vegetation. Here, much like casting to a permit, let your fly sink to the bottom in front of the fish and then strip it in hops, to indicate a fleeing, hiding crab.

There are many acceptable crab patterns out there, but I have found that a brown Clouser or lead-eyed fly tied with a piece of palmer-wound fur strip works fine. A wiggling action and a near-bottom presentation are your keys to success. I'll probably stir up a lot of disagreement on this one, but I don't bother to use a crab fly unless I can see the fish I'm throwing it to. I simply believe that stripers prefer a soft, oily fish, if it's available—so that's the kind of fly I prospect with, even if I know there are crabs on the bottom. Keep in mind that the water must be quite shallow if you're to see the bottom; thus the crabs you'll imitate are likely to be fairly small. I see little sense in attempting to develop large crab or lobster flies.

Figure 17c   Sand fiddler crab.

Other Baitfish

I'm certain that some of you will think me remiss for not listing as prime striper food such bait as eels, mackerel, flounders, spot, whiting, and lobsters. Remember, however, that stripers will feed on nearly everything they can fit into their mouths. To be listed in this book, I feel that a bait should be easy to imitate with a fly—both in appearance and behavior. For instance, you can make a lovely eel with a piece of black or olive fur strip. But eels crawl along the bottom—how can you realistically duplicate that? I also feel that to be considered a key forage, a bait should be one that stripers might home in on to the exclusion of all others. **Flounders,** for example, are almost impossible to see, and while stripers do eat them, they are unlikely to be in such abundance anywhere today that stripers will work on them to the exclusion of other available forage. Another example is the **spot,** a small drum common in the mid-Atlantic and often found in the stomachs of Chesapeake Bay stripers. Once, while casting to a huge school of stripers near the Chesapeake Bay Bridge Tunnel, I readily caught bass on a 4-inch white Groceries. Those bass that I kept contained spot—but also similar-size menhaden. A white Deceiver worked well as a representation of either bait. Indeed, there are several good general-purpose flies—Deceivers, fur-strips, and Clousers—that, tied in the appropriate thickness and length, will successfully suggest a variety of possible prey species. Let's face it: If stripers were so discerning that your flies must always exactly duplicate prey species, they probably wouldn't hit a bunch of feathers in the first place.

While there are many potential species of baitfish along the stripers' range, tie or buy some flies detailed for specific location. You can't beat local fly shops for knowledge of a given area. There may also be regular striper blitzes in particular spots that concentrate on a baitfish I haven't listed here. While I'm confident that one of the five types of flies that I discuss in chapter 6 will do the job, you may also end up with your own favorite patterns. I hope so: Studying stripers' feeding habits then developing flies and presentation techniques is half the fun of fly fishing for stripers.

PART II

Equipment

CHAPTER 4

Fly Rods, Reels, and Lines

Imeet a lot of people who are interested in striper fishing but haven't gotten started because they're afraid their freshwater equipment won't be adequate. This simply isn't true, however—at least not on the entry level. While your slow-action, 6-weight trout rod will not throw a heavy sinking-head line and a #4/0 Groceries fly, that's not the way you'll start striper fishing anyway. In protected waters, from both beach and boat, a 6- or 7-weight outfit with floating and sinking-tip lines and some of your freshwater tapered leaders cut back to 12-pound test will do nicely. Quiet waters yield mostly smaller bass, along with the occasional larger fish.

This is not to say, however, that there isn't a whole world of specialized fly tackle available to enhance your efficiency and enjoyment of the sport—because there is. But you can get started with what you have, and grow into the extras if you get hooked. As you read this chapter, don't be intimidated if you don't already own a lot of the equipment I'll discuss. Get started instead by fishing for the schoolies along protected beaches or in tidal rivers. Like a lot of things in life, setting your sights on self-improvement goals—improved casting, fishing prowess, or possessing top equipment—and then striving to achieve these is much of the fun.

Rods

I recently gave away the last of what I thought of as my "old rods." A couple of 10-year-old fiberglass and graphite composite rods had sat in my rod rack for years. I looked them over annually when I cleaned my good rods for the winter, and finally the realization hit me that I would go out and buy a new rod before I would use one of these old noodles, even for one tide.

The difference between today's rod technology and that of 10 years ago is stunning. Yes, you can make adjustments in your timing and cast with the old stuff, but one of the latest generation of graphite rods feels like a feather in the hand, and has a quick resilience that effortlessly builds line speed. These newer rods are designed to handle the heavier lines and larger flies that often add to your productivity when striped bass fly fishing. And frankly, I'm amazed at the prices, on both ends of the spectrum. Without question, what is selling today for over $500 is excellent, but excellent rods can also be purchased for well under half that price, with long warrantees included. This is not to say that you don't get anything for the extra money; you do. You get refinements that are relevant to very discerning casters, or to those who simply want to own the best. I don't know where fly rods are going from here, but I know that anglers on virtually every budget can fish today with a great-casting rod.

I have already intimated that I like light, fast rods. Here's why. Striper fishing is not like southern flats fishing, in which the tarpon artillery may not move off the deck for hours at a time. When you're striper fishing you will be constantly casting, searching every pocket and rip line, knowing that a strike is possible on any cast. Your rod should thus be comfortable to cast, and lightness, especially in the heavier line weights, helps with this a lot. Also, the need to cast fully dressed flies in windy conditions can come up at any time. By going up one or even two line weights, you add a line density that will carry heavier flies and be less affected by the wind. Why not simply cast these lines on the rods that are rated for them? Because such rods are normally much heavier than you'd want to throw for hours on end. Fast-action rods still perform very well when casting lines heavier than they're actually rated for; often they perform better than older, slower rods that are factory rated for the heavier line. Also, some casters don't care for what they perceive as the "harsh" feel of a fast-action rod, but going up a line weight or two will slow the rod down, making it a bit more forgiving if your timing isn't always right on the money. Others simply prefer the feel of a slower rod, which loads more deeply into its butt section. Again, this feeling can be to some degree attained in a fast-action rod by "lining it up" a weight or two. You may also want to drop down to the original line weight in some situations, to get the high-line-speed and tight-loop type of performance that fast-action rods are capable of.

If you fish a lot, you'll ideally have a whole stable of rods. This is, of course, not practical for everyone. Nonetheless, I've prepared a list of the rods and line weights that are best suited to tossing the flies that represent the striper's prime forage. One caution as you read this information: When I suggest several rod weights, and several Superhead or line weights, use the heavier weight rods with the heavier lines and vice versa. For example, don't use a 450-grain head on an 8-weight rod; while I don't believe you'd break the rod, its performance would be poor. L.L. Bean has a special Fly-Fishing Hotline at 1-800-FISH-LLB (1-800-347-4552); call with these kinds of questions about any of its products.

Bunker flies and large Groceries   11- or 12-weight rod; 550-grain or heavier Superhead. No floating or intermediate lines are recommended for casting these highly wind-resistant flies.

Groceries flies and very heavily dressed Deceivers   10- or 11-weight rod; 350-, 450- (450 is the maximum for a 10-weight), or 550-grain Superheads; 11- through 13-weight floating or intermediate lines.

Deceivers and most intermediate-size flies   8-, 9-, or 10-weight rods; 350- (maximum for 8- or 9-weight) or 450-grain Superheads; 8 through 11 floating or intermediate lines.

Juves, Clousers, and most smaller flies   6-, 7-, or 8-weight rods; 250- (maximum for 6- or 7-weight) or 350-grain Superheads; 6 through 9 floating or intermediate lines.

While the ability to cast flies with various amounts of wind resistance and to handle sinking lines of different weights are prime considerations for me when I choose my rod weight, fish fighting is also an issue. I have caught stripers into the mid-30-inch range on four weights, but I hadn't planned to. You can usually almost straight-line a fish—fighting it with only the very butt of your rod and putting on all the pressure that your reel seat and leader can handle. During many fights, however, there are times when the fish is just under your boat, and you need a rod with lifting power. As a rule of thumb, I use at least a 10-weight if there is any chance that fish of over 20 pounds are present; I go below an 8-weight only to fish for what I know will be fish under the mid-20-inch range. Day in and day out you will put too much strain on your tackle and overtire fish if you go too far outside these guidelines.

I'm a notorious breaker of fly rods, though not often on fish. I've fallen on them in rough water, caught them in trolling motors and regular motors, shut lockers and

Figure 18   Rod-on-reel case.

doors on them, stepped on them, cast them into T-tops, broken ferrules casting them, and had other incidents that I've thankfully forgotten. Indeed, rods are most frequently broken by accident. The more fishing you do and the more you transport your rods, the more likely these accidents are to occur. Here is one tip that will eliminate most such problems: Get what L.L. Bean calls a "rod-on-reel case" (Fig. 18). Break down the rod into two pieces, hook the fly on a guide, and the whole outfit, still strung, will slide into a protected tube with a padded reel pouch. These are made to hold either one or two rods. Take yours right out on the boat with you, and keep the rod that you're not using inside it. Your rod will be ready to go in seconds, and you won't have any accidents.

At the end of the season I inspect all of my rods; have them repaired, if necessary; and prepare them for storage. First, clean the rod with soap and water, and use a soft brush to thoroughly clean the cork handle. Inspect the guides for line-fraying cracks, grooves, and frayed windings. With WD-40 and an old toothbrush, clean all the guides and metal parts thoroughly. Wax the graphite surfaces with an automotive wax. Stand the rod on its butt for the winter, taking it apart if necessary; don't store the rod with any bend in it.

I also wash my rods with warm soap and water after every trip, and I'm still using some six-year-old graphite rods that have now been fishing over 400 times. They perform like they did when they were new.

Reels

I feel about fly reels much the way I do about rods: The quality and selection available today are superb. Rods, I envision, will always wear out or otherwise become obsolete. Reels, on the other hand, can last for generations. The basic concept of the direct-drive fly reel has changed very little over time. There have, however, been many excellent improvements of late. One of my biggest concerns is the stability of the zillion new reel manufacturers on the market. We need the innovations that these people bring to the industry, but if I'm going to shell out several hundred dollars for a bar-stock reel, I want to be confident that I can get a gear to replace one that fails 10 years from now. I'm confident that L.L. Bean will be around years from now to honor its guarantee of customer satisfaction.

There are a few terms that you should understand in order to evaluate reels. A **click drag** offers minimal resistance; it's simply a little piece of metal that's held by a spring and clicks against a gear attached to the spool. On the other hand, a **disc-drag** reel employs an actual braking surface that is capable of resisting the fish as it pulls line from the reel during a run. The considerable range of adjustments you can make to the tension of the disc drag allows you to compensate for leader strength and/or the size of the fish. Even though only a small percentage of stripers take out line against the drag, some of them do big time, so a disc drag is a must for an all-around striper reel. **Antireverse** is a feature that prevents the handle from turning backward and rapping you in the knuckles, even when the spool is revolving and paying out line. Reel frames are either cast from a mold or milled out of a piece of solid bar stock. They all work if taken care of, but a one-piece cast model is more solid than one that is screwed together, and the bar-stock types are improvements over the cast. Some reels are painted, some are anodized. An anodized surface stands up to salt water far better than a painted. The price goes up with each stage of improvement.

That said, your first concern in purchasing a new striper reel should be its size. If there is one common mistake that I see people make, it is buying a reel that is too big. Big reels are heavier than small ones, and every time that you cast you have to move that weight around. Matching the physical size of your reel to your rod is also a consideration. Place too small a reel on a big rod and it will feel out of balance. As a general rule, I follow the manufacturer's recommendations as to which rod a reel should be used on. Sometimes a manufacturer recommends a reel for use with a 9- or 10-weight line; I would confidently use this reel on a 10-weight rod. One of the reasons that I feel this way is the advent of Spectra backing material. I've used Spectra (a very strong synthetic fiber) for years: 30-pound test on outfits up to 9-weight or so, and 50-pound test on anything larger. The first reel on which I ever used Spectra backing was a multiplying reel rated for an 8- or 9-weight line that I wanted to use for bonito, fish that require some serious backing. The reel was rated to hold 220 yards of 20-pound-test Dacron. A friend gave me a 300-yard spool of 35-pound-test Spectra, though, and I dumped the whole thing on the reel, along with the recommended 8-weight floating line. Twice the strength, half again the line capacity—that's what Spectra will do for you. Just two cautions: Most knots greatly reduce its breaking strength. Use a Bimini twist (see page 54) and Pliobond all the wraps, since Spectra also tends to come untied. Yes, I've heard people talk about the line binding into the spool under drag pressure. I've seen no evidence of this on the line strengths that I'm suggesting, and I've really tried to do it. My second caution is that Spectra is thin, and when you're tight to a big fish (or anything else) it can easily cut you if you try to squeeze it between your fingers for extra drag pressure.

Your next concern should be the style and action of the reel. Your options here are multiplier, large-arbor, direct-drive, and antireverse reels. In a **multiplier** reel one revolution of the handle, through gearing, turns the spool more than one revolution; line can thus be more rapidly retrieved. I like the multiplier concept, especially for bonito and albacore, which have a tendency to swim at warp speed right for the boat. Stripers, however, seldom move toward you fast enough to present difficulties in keeping up. Another side of this issue is that on the multiplier I've used, the gearing subjects the handle to some odd torque, and the reel feels like it's binding when I apply pressure to the handle against the pull of a fish. Also, there isn't much of a selection of multipliers on the market as of this writing.

Another approach to rapid line retrieve is the **large-arbor** concept. In a large-arbor reel the spool is of greater diameter; when it revolves, it thus picks up more line per revolution. The spool is also typically wider so that a fish can pull away more backing or fly line before the spool diameter shrinks. Preserving the larger-diameter spool also preserves retrieval speed. A large-arbor reel doesn't require the gearing used in a multiplier, and when it's used with Spectra backing a high speed of retrieve is maintained (runoffs change the spool diameter less than if thicker Dacron was your backing)—though still not as high as the multiplier. Large-arbor reels, as of this writing, are typically a high-end product. You can get some of the same effect by buying the larger-diameter reel of the models that you are considering.

I own mostly **direct-drive** reels, though I do have a couple of high-end **antireverse** models. In the latter the handle is not attached directly to the reel spool. Instead, the handle's connection to the spool is channeled through a device that will not turn backward—often a gear and dog or a one-way bearing. The spool is connected to all of this through the disc drag so that the spool can turn backward to let out line, but the handle cannot. In general I find that direct drive is fine. It is possible, however, for a big fish to catch you with your fingers too comfortably clutching the handle, and break you off with a shake of its head. An antireverse reel prevents this from happening if the drag is properly set. If I'm ever to hook the world-record striper (oh God, please!), I'd like it to be on an antireverse reel. The downsides to antireverse reels are that unless you have a fair amount of drag pressure dialed in, you get nowhere when you reel, and you may not realize it. Some anglers really dislike this characteristic. Antireverse reels are also more complicated internally, and weigh a bit more. Given the excellent reels being made today, however, I've had no problems with reliability, and the extra weight is minimal. Like large arbors, antireverse reels tend to be quite pricey.

How expensive a reel do I need? I caught several hundred stripers (of up to 27 inches) this past summer in a Cape Cod salt pond using a 5-weight rod and an L.L. Bean click-drag trout reel. The water was less than 4 feet deep, and many of these fish took 100 feet of backing. I just love fishing with this outfit. The reel has a list price of $95. On the other hand I also used an expensive bar-stock reel on a 10-weight rod to land many stripers of over 30 inches—and quite a few over 40—among the rocks of the Elizabeth Islands and in Maine's fast-flowing Kennebec River. My inexpensive reel would never have taken the kind of heat that I applied to those brutes as I steered them away from the boulder-infested shorelines. For the heavy-duty end of striper

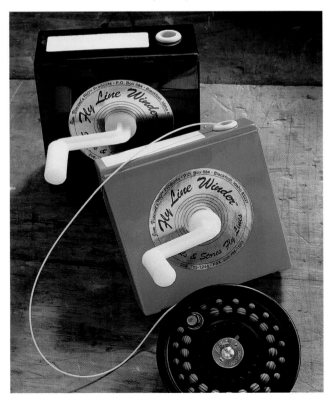

fishing, you need at least a middle-of-the-road-priced reel with a solid disc-drag system. You'll also need this reel for shore fishing if larger fish are around. What you get for your money is a bit more obvious with reels than with rods. The difference between a $150 cast reel that is perfectly adequate and a $450 bar-stock reel that turns like a jeweled watch is clear when you handle the two. The stripers, however, don't know or care which one you're holding.

One consideration that may come up is the spare spool. I used to routinely purchase a spare spool with every reel. Because I have so many reels and lines, though, I now

Figure 19   Fly-line winder. (Photo by L.L. Bean)

use the Rio line-winder system (Fig. 19). This system is comprised of a comparatively inexpensive spool that slips inside a box with a small hole in the center of each side. You place the spool inside the box, insert a crank (which is sold separately) through the hole, and reel your fly line on or off your reel. These spools can be stored in their own box and take up less room than most reel spools. But I do still use reel spools, especially for a quick change in the field. Some of the more expensive reels, however, have spools that are difficult to change in the field, and each one may cost as much as a reel. Still, a spare spool can be handy, especially if you own only one or two reels. Get the salesman to show you how the spool is changed and see how easy or difficult he finds it, or if there's any potential for small but critical parts to suddenly abandon ship.

In the winter, I take the fly lines off my spools and clip off the backing knot. I wash each reel and, after drying, go over the outside with WD-40 and a toothbrush. I also take the spool out and put a drop of grease here and there, where I can see it belongs. I spray the interior with WD-40 but perform no further disassembly, since I don't trust my mechanical ability. Several of my reels are still working well after 10 years of this simple maintenance routine and plenty of use.

Fly Lines

There is a truly bewildering array of fly lines available to the saltwater fly fisher. One of the biggest problems that this creates is the one I have now: It can be time consuming to decide which lines I want to fish with, and which I want to have as spares, and then to rig the four or five active rods that I might take with me for a full day on the water.

All the lines that I'll discuss here are **weight forward,** which means that a heavy section called the **head** is in the forward portion of the line; this is followed by a longer, thinner section called the **running line.** The weight of the head portion determines the weight number of the rod for which the whole line is made. A line labeled as a 9-weight, for instance, has a head—defined as the first 30 feet of line—that weighs 9 grains per foot, or 270 grains.

Floating lines, in order to achieve the required weight while still using a material that by necessity is lighter than water, have a much fatter head than do sinking-head lines of the same weight. Thus floating lines offer more wind resistance and take up more space on the reel. Nonetheless, they're important for several kinds of presentations; I use them a lot for fishing in estuaries and shallow beaches, usually with small flies. Clear floating lines may also have their place in clear-water and very shallow flats situations, although I haven't yet tried them.

Floating lines come in several tapers—for wind, for distance, and for delicacy. All are built to serve an extreme need. The very short, heavy tapers made for turning over into the wind will hurt your distance in light air and land indelicately. Conversely, the lines made exclusively for long-distance casts have a very long head that takes forever to work out of the guides. A short, fast taper is a good general-purpose compromise that keeps false casting to a minimum, increasing your productivity. I buy the L.L. Bean GQS Series floating lines; I can't distinguish their quality from lines that cost twice as much.

The bulk of my striper fishing and almost all of my big bass fishing, however, is done with **sinking** lines. These sink at a uniform speed. They start with the intermediate type, which sinks at the rate of an inch or two per second, and increase through several stages of increasingly rapid sinking speeds. Only the intermediate is widely used in striper fishing; because it is denser than a floating line, it casts better yet is still easy to pick out of the water. For a lot of beach fishing in water that's over wading depth but under 10 feet (this fits a lot of beaches), intermediates drop just below surface disturbances and work well. You can even fish a surface fly on an intermediate, if you don't wait too long before you start your retrieve. On the other hand, if you cast upcurrent using a weighted fly, and then allow a little sinking time before your retrieve, you can fish several feet under the water with an intermediate. If you're just starting out, this is the line you *must* have. I do a lot of casting from a boat toward shallow rocky shorelines during low light, when big bass are still in tight to the beach. I use a 12-weight rod with a 13-weight intermediate line to make long casts with some large flies. I find the heavyweight intermediate perfect. There are also several clear intermediates, some of which my exclusively shore-fishing friends like beach guide Kenny Vanderlaske swear by. I have experimented with these quite a bit and can see no difference in terms of scaring fish, but they do have monofilament cores, and tend to tangle worse in cold water than do vinyl-covered nylon lines. L.L. Bean offers both sinking and floating fly lines made specifically for different water temperatures. I have tested some of these, especially the cold-water lines, and found them to be less problematic in the cooler waters of the Northeast.

The level of full-sinking line just beyond intermediate is the type II, which probably has some application for fishing windy beaches and high surf. I haven't tried these, but I plan to. For faster sinking rates than this, I believe that you should be looking at rapid-sinking-head designs like the Superhead series. These have long (by sinking-tip standards) sinking heads—25 feet—of dense material. The heads are weighted in grains, making it easy to determine how they will perform on a given rod weight. They are joined abruptly, like shooting heads, to a thin running line. Super-heads, therefore, cast like shooting heads (see chapter 9). I still use regular sinking tips some, and they work in a lot of situations, but Superheads cast better and stay deeper during the retrieve because they're longer. For most anglers they have replaced lines in which only the tip sinks. In fact, I know several very experienced fly-fishing boat guides who use nothing but this type of line; they don't even carry

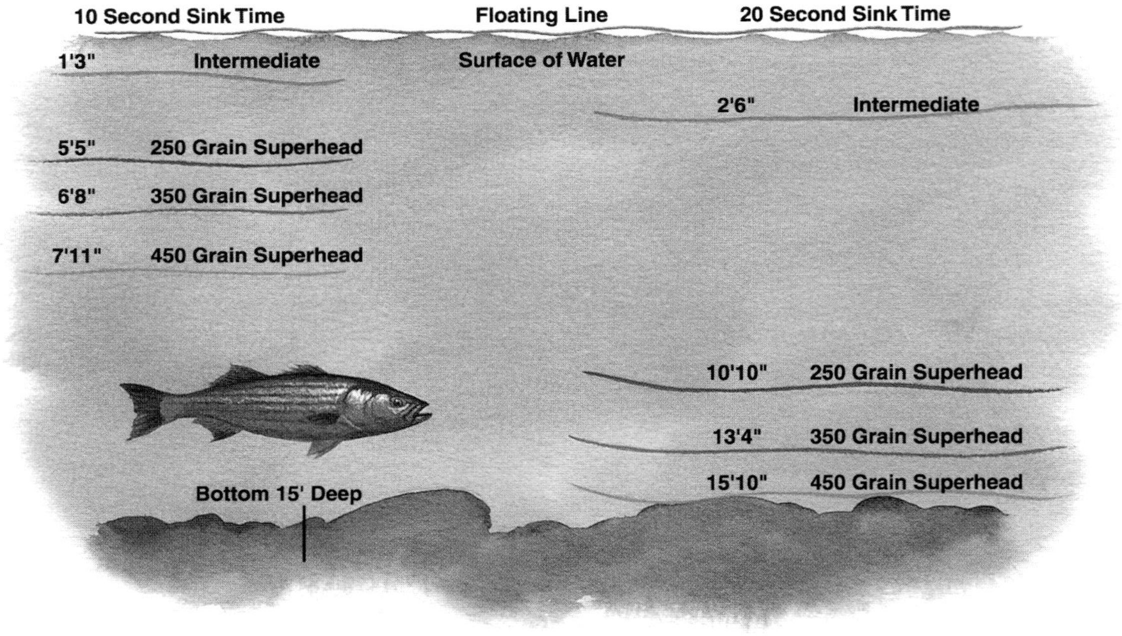

10 Second Sink Time		Floating Line	20 Second Sink Time	
1'3"	Intermediate	Surface of Water		
			2'6"	Intermediate
5'5"	250 Grain Superhead			
6'8"	350 Grain Superhead			
7'11"	450 Grain Superhead			
			10'10"	250 Grain Superhead
			13'4"	350 Grain Superhead
Bottom 15' Deep			15'10"	450 Grain Superhead

Figure 20   Sink depth achieved by various fly lines in 10- and 20-second sink times.

floating or intermediate lines on board. If you plan to use a boat for stripers, you're going to want a Superhead-type line. Superheads sink at the rate of approximately 5 inches per second for a 150-grain head; this rate increases by about 1.5 inches per second for every additional 100 grains of weight. This isn't the whole story, though. One of the reasons that the first 150 grains sink more than twice as fast as the next 100 is that the increased diameter of the thicker line has drag in the water as it sinks. Conversely, when you retrieve, this resistance helps keep the larger fly line down in the water column—deeper than you could maintain with a smaller-diameter line of the same weight (Fig. 20).

Some anglers use a **shooting-head** system to allow them to quickly change from one head to another. You can buy many different kinds of running lines and even more kinds of heads, including everything that I've mentioned here. Typically the two are attached loop to loop, with loops that you fasten onto the ends of both running line and head. You need only the running line on your reel and a wallet of shooting heads. This system sounds great, and if a few things that I'm about to point out don't bother you, it may be your answer. However, I fish a lot, and I make many casts each time I go. I never know when my loop connections might get weak and break, and I don't yet trust them. Also, with many shooting-head combos the thinner running line cannot transfer enough energy to create a good loop in the head. The result is that only the head and a few feet of running line called the overhang can be kept outside the rod tip—and in some wind conditions I prefer to false cast more or less line than this limitation would dictate. Finally, I have experimented with shooting heads quite a bit, and I find the loop-to-loop connection area unpleasant to contend with; it works all right, I just find it clunky.

Whatever your fly line, it needs maintenance. Stretch it just before use. Keep it clean and lubricated. You'll also need to regularly troll it behind a boat or from a bridge, or twirl it in the air, to take out the inevitable twists caused by casting.

At a bare minimum clean your lines every few trips; use one of the pads made just for this task and some mild soap and warm water. Rinse each line thoroughly, wipe it dry, then dress it with one of the silicone line dressings on the market. In a six-hour fishing trip I may throw hundreds of casts, and I'll dress my line two or three times. As I boat between fishing spots, I occasionally clip off my fly and troll the bare line behind my craft. It is even more important to dress and untwist your line at the end of the day, so that it doesn't kink or dry out on the reel. A quick untwisting can be performed by noting the direction in which your line is twisting and then twirling the head in the air in the opposite

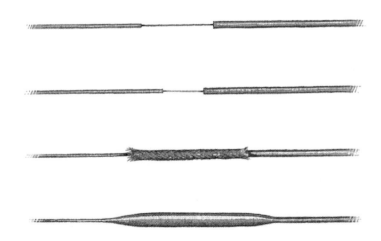

Figure 21　Braided mono line repair.

direction. (Maybe someday we'll be able to look back on this maintenance nostalgi-
cally, the way we now look back on the rinsing and air-drying of linen lines common
60 years ago.)

After serious use of any fly line, the line coating in your head-to-running-line
junction may crack. Nicks from rocks can also cut through the coating, as can the
point of your hook. Or you may tear it when you try to pick the tangles from your
running line. There are two excellent cures for these maladies. If the wound is
small, clean and dry your line in this area, and put a dab of Pliobond on the crack;
for fly-line illness, Pliobond is the wonder drug. If a serious separation takes place,
especially at the head-to-running-line connection (I've seen the coating separate 2
inches on fairly new lines), use a piece of braided mono to cover the area (Fig. 21).
Braided mono comes in various pound-test ratings, all of them are strong enough
to replace a fly-line core; either the 30- or 40-pound-test size will probably do the
job. The braid holds by the Chinese handcuff concept. Push one end of the fly line
into one end of a 3- or 4-inch piece of braided mono. Once it's started, push a short
distance of the braid onto the end of the fly line, while you hold onto the fly line
just above it with your other hand. After the whole piece has been worked onto the
line you can easily slide it along the entire length of a fly line. Straddle the wound
with this section of braid, allowing at least 1½ inches of braid to extend out onto
the coated fly line on each side of the rift. With your fingers, smooth the braid out
tightly in both directions. Apply a liberal coat of the wonder drug, and let it dry.
Then trim the errant fibers that will curl up at the ends of the braid, and apply one
more coat to them. Better than new! I've got a couple of older lines from which I
cut the damaged section of original material (including the core) and replaced it
entirely with braided mono. In 1997 I caught my biggest bass of the year—a 44-
inch fish—on one of these lines. I've never had this connection method fail, and it's
very smooth.

Whenever I set up a new line, I use a system that Brock Apfel showed me to
remember which line is which. I label each line's end—the one that attaches to the
backing—with a
waterproof marker.
I use a long dash to

Figure 22   13-weight.

signify five, and a short dot for every additional one (Fig. 22). I use the aforemen-
tioned Rio system to hold all of my lines, and I label the spools by writing on them
with the same waterproof marker. This makes it possible to carry extra lines into the
field, where they can be changed in minutes. Be careful how tightly you wind the

lines onto the spools; the sides will crack later if you do so too tightly. Wind the head of the line on first, so that it will be ready to wind right onto your reel.

Backing

In the section on reels I made my case for using Spectra as a backing material, but whether I use Spectra or Dacron, my connection process is the same. Nail-knot (see page 53) a section of 40-pound-test monofilament line onto the end of your fly line's running line. Tie a small double surgeon's loop (see page 56) in the end of the mono.

In the end of your backing tie a Bimini twist (see page 54), and *only* a Bimini twist. Make sure that the loop is approximately 2 feet long. Cut the end of the loop, and smooth any twists out of the tag ends. Double the two strands over into a loop (a double-strand loop approximately 1 foot in length), and tie with a double surgeon's knot. Coat the knots with Pliobond. The double-line loop in your backing is now easily big enough to connect to the loop on the end of your fly line by passing the whole Rio spool right through the loop in your backing. A double thickness of Spectra has never done any perceptible damage to either kind of mono loop on the end of my fly line. I use this system for my freshwater equipment also.

An alternative approach that I'll try next season uses a braided-mono loop just larger than what you'd use on a butt leader (Fig. 23). Instructions for making a braided-mono loop and attaching it to your backing are found on page 61.

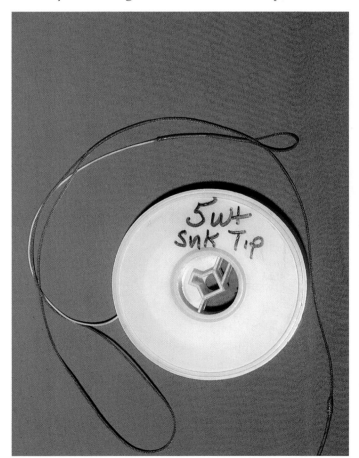

Figure 23   The braided mono loop attached to the backing goes through the loop on the end of the fly line and around the spool for quick connection.

C H A P T E R 5

Knots and Leaders

here have been some excellent books written just on tying knots, and I've learned a lot from reading them. There are, however, only a half-dozen knots necessary to fly fish for stripers. When you tie any of these knots use your thumb and index finger to hold the point where two lines are pinched or twisted together, and use plenty of saliva to lubricate the knot before you draw it up tight. Refer to the diagrams to help you learn these knots.

Nail Knot

The nail knot is the basic knot for attaching mono to fly lines (Fig. 24). Lay the mono against the fly line, with its tag end pointed up the line. Squeeze the line and

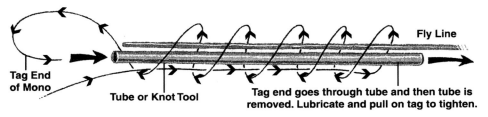

Figure 24   Nail or tube knot.

mono together at the point where you want the knot to start, then wrap the mono in a backward direction for about eight turns, around itself, the fly line, and a small nail, tube, or tool (like the L.L. Bean knot tool). Now slide the tag end back through the wrapped area (this is where the tool comes in), remove the knot tool, lubricate, and carefully pull tight by pulling on the tag end and the standing mono. Make sure that each wrap lies smoothly beside the next, with no wraps crossed. The fly line is merely sandwiched in the middle. I apply Pliobond to all my nail knots.

The Bimini Twist

The Bimini twist is simply the best loop knot that you can tie in either Dacron or Spectra (Fig. 25). There are those that would argue that this is also true of mono. The spider hitch, which I'll cover next, is, however, much simpler to tie, and according to some big-game experts like Captain Dave Preble, it's just as good. Captain Preble has written a book or two on tuna fishing and is the kind of guy who would be sure of his opinions before he gave them out. In testing, I've broken lots of Biminis

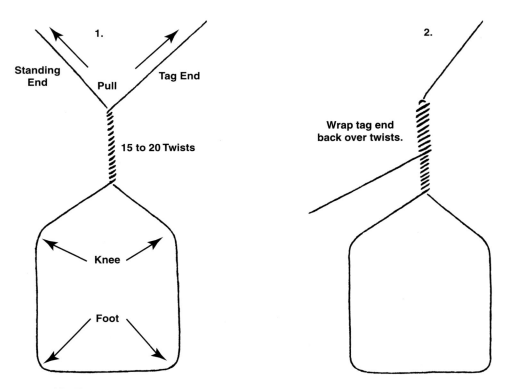

Figure 25   Bimini twist.

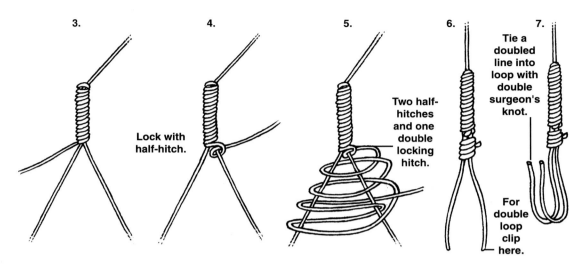

Figure 25   Bimini twist.

with spider hitches, although just as frequently the line breaks away from any knots. In Dacron, however, the spider hitch greatly reduces the breaking strength, while the Bimini does not.

Sitting in a chair with your feet on the floor and knees slightly bent, pass the line down around the bottom of your feet, and out around both knees. Pass the tag end over the standing line and, pulling lightly on the standing line, wrap the tag end around the standing line 20 times. Pull on both lines, forcing the 20 wraps to become tight twists and moving the connection down against your knees. Squeeze the junction of the line with the thumb and finger of one hand so that the twists will not come undone. With your other hand, wrap the standing end tightly back over the twists until you reach the point down by your knees where both lines separate. Tie the tag end around the line on one side of the loop with a half hitch, then do the same around the other. Now tie three successive half hitches around both the lines together, each farther down the loop and lying neatly against the last. Finish by tying a knot that looks like a half hitch, but in which the tag end goes three times around both lines of the loop. These last four knots are simply to keep the tag end of the knot from unraveling, and I therefore coat this area with Pliobond.

To make the double loop that I like for the backing connection and my boat leaders, clip the loop in the center and run each tag end through your fingers to remove any twists. Fold the doubled line back over, forming a loop, and tie the loop with a double surgeon's knot.

Spider Hitch

Form a loop of doubled line (Fig. 26). Lay the loop over one index finger with all but 4 inches hanging down toward the floor. Squeeze the tag end of the line between the thumb and forefinger of your other hand. Reach down with that hand, and also grab between the same thumb and index finger the lines hanging down toward the ground, from the index finger of your other hand. At this point the index finger of one hand should be at one end of a double-line loop, and your other hand should have all four strands tucked between thumb and forefinger. Next twist your index finger inside the loop in a circle four times, twisting the four strands together as you go. Reaching with the fingertips of the hand holding the four strands, grab the point where the twisted lines come together so that the loop that they have formed around your index finger won't unravel. Remove your index finger from the loop created by the twisting. This is much easier than it sounds. Once learned, everything I've discussed so far can be done with your eyes closed in 10 or 15 seconds. Now pass the long original loop through the same eye that your index finger was in. It is absolutely key at this point that you thoroughly lubricate the knot before you proceed. Holding the apex of the long loop in one hand and squeezing the standing line and tag end in the other, tighten the knot. Be careful that you do not use the lubricated state of this knot to overtighten and weaken it. Pull slowly only until it's firm. The resulting loop can be made small for use on tippets, or longer to create a double line to tie on shock leaders. The L.L. Bean knot card shows you an alternative way to tie this knot: Wrap coils around your thumb and then pass the double line through them.

Double Surgeon's Knot

The double surgeon's can be used either to make a loop or to tie two pieces of line together (Fig. 27). Pass the doubled lines loosely over themselves, creating a loop, then pass the ends out through this loop. Go through the loop twice for a double surgeon's. Lubricate the lines thoroughly and pull slowly on all four strands until tight. This knot has considerably less breaking strength than some, but you are safe when you use it on anything over 20-pound test, since you can't put that much pressure on with a fly rod anyway.

To make a double surgeon's loop, just double over the end of the line in which you want the loop and then tie a double surgeon's knot in the doubled line. Because of the double surgeon's loop's inferior breaking strength I use it to make a loop on the

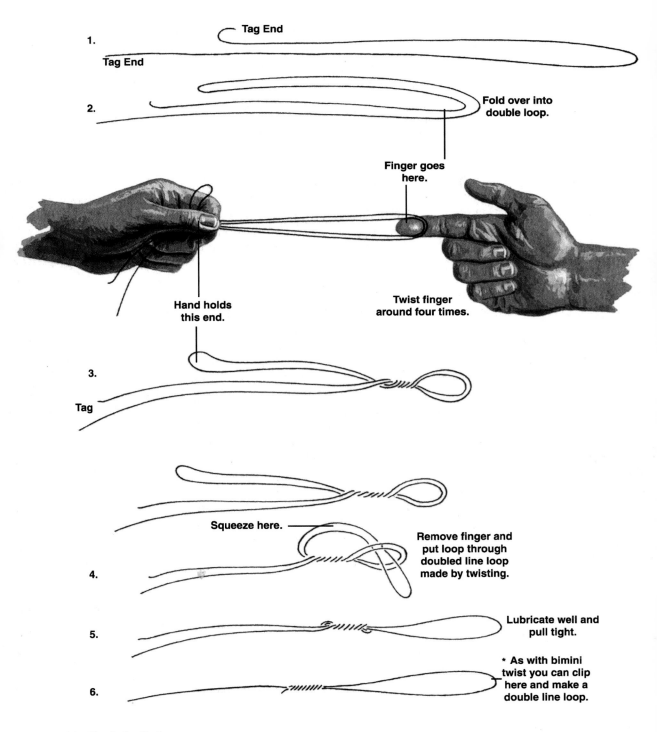

1. **Tag End**

   Tag End

2. **Fold over into double loop.**

   Finger goes here.

   Hand holds this end.

   Twist finger around four times.

3. **Tag**

4. **Squeeze here.**

   Remove finger and put loop through doubled line loop made by twisting.

5. **Lubricate well and pull tight.**

6. *** As with bimini twist you can clip here and make a double line loop.**

Figure 26   The Spider Hitch.

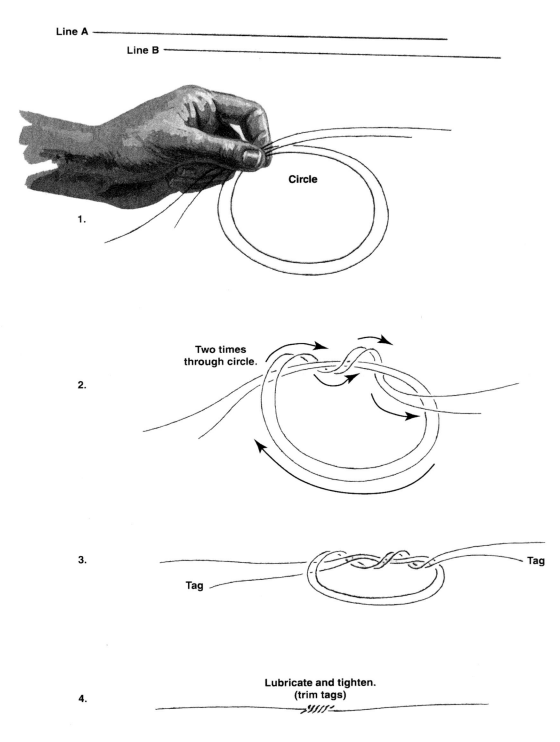

Figure 27   Double surgeon's knot.

end of my 20-pound-test leader sections—however, I use the slower-to-tie but superior spider hitch on the 15- and 12-pound-test tippets. Some advocate a triple surgeon's (three times through the loop), but I have found this to be no stronger than the double.

Duncan Loop

I love this knot because I can tie it at night without seeing it, and it makes a lovely loop (Fig. 28). I use it to attach flies, but part of it can also be used to attach two lines, like extra backing, by tying the knotted part of the Duncan loop over the other standing line, and vice versa. The Duncan loop, even properly tied, can slip and pull down tight. If you are concerned about this you can first tie a loose overhand knot in the tippet material, and then put the line through first the eye of the hook, and then that knot; finally, pull everything tight against the eye of the fly, then tie a Duncan loop knot just above it. When pulled tight, the Duncan knot will slide up against the overhand knot, and a loop will form at the fly that cannot be pulled down.

To tie a Duncan loop, pass your tippet through the eye of the fly and pull out 5 inches of tag end. Lay this tag end along the standing line and squeeze the two together with one hand, about 2 inches in front of the fly. Bend the tag end back toward the hook eye. Now, using your thumb and middle finger, squeeze it against the other two lines 1/2 inch from the eye, leaving a couple of inches of tag end and a slight loop. With the index fingertip of the hand near the fly, pass the tag end around the double line and out through the loop four or five times. After the final pass out through the loop, grasp the tag end and pull the knot loosely together. At this stage, the size of the loop attached to the fly can be adjusted by simply sliding the knot back and forth on the standing line. Set the loop where you want it (usually snug against the hook eye), knowing that it will expand considerably as the knot is finally tightened. Lubricate very well—as with the spider hitch, lubricating the knot is key—and pull tight. If you want no loop at all (a locked-down knot), you can have it just by pulling everything tight against the hook eye. This has become the knot that I use to tie on flies, from #16 Wulffs to #6/0 bunker flies, 99 percent of the time.

Leaders

Once, during the heat of a striper blitz, Brock Apfel tied a Groceries fly directly to the end of his 40-pound-test butt leader, only a few inches from his fly line. The

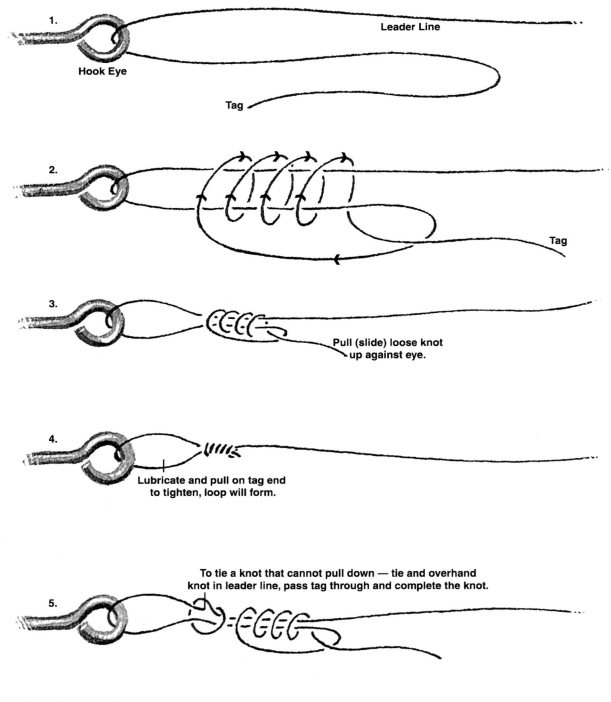

1.

Leader Line

Hook Eye

Tag

2.

Tag

3.

Pull (slide) loose knot
up against eye.

4.

Lubricate and pull on tag end
to tighten, loop will form.

To tie a knot that cannot pull down — tie and overhand
knot in leader line, pass tag through and complete the knot.

5.

Figure 28   Duncan loop.

bass took his fly without hesitation. There may in fact be occasions when a long, fine leader is necessary to catch stripers, but I've never witnessed them.

Nonetheless, I'm sure that having some length of clear, hard-to-detect, monofilament leader material between the fly and the fly line is necessary for consistent fishing. Besides, there are other considerations, like your ability to turn over a small fly, and having something other than your fly line to withstand the abrasion caused by a big bass trying to rub your fly out on a rock. You also need a butt leader (a thick piece of leader material that is permanently attached to your fly line) to attach your regular leaders to, since you will need to change them regularly.

Butt Leaders

As a material for my butt leaders I still haven't completely decided between a piece of heavy mono nail-knotted onto the fly line and a piece of braided mono. The braided mono makes a smoother, neater connection, and it holds onto the fly line over an area of several inches. The nail knot, even if tied with 8 or 10 turns, can yank the coating off the fly line and fail. This happened to me last summer on a big bass that took my fly at boatside. The tiny strands of braided mono can, however, become brittle and break, as can the strand of heavy mono—I'm not sure in which case it will happen more quickly. I change all of my butt leaders on lines that see any action at least annually. Given the apparent benefits, I plan to convert the rest of my lines to braided-mono butt leaders this winter; I mention both methods only because using a piece of heavy, nail-knotted mono is a method that has stood the test of time.

You can buy braided-mono butt leaders with loops. The leaders are, however, shorter than I like, and the loops are formed with superglue—which forms a hard, brittle spot that can cause the braid to break at the point where it is glued. I prefer to make my own (Fig. 29). Slip a piece of braided mono (30-pound test on lines to 8-weight, 40-pound test on lines 9-weight and above) onto the fly line as described in the section on fly-line repair (see page 50), and push it up the line about 2 inches. Coat the fly line–braid connection thoroughly with Pliobond. After the first coat dries you may need to trim the ends of the braid to make them flush with the fly line, then give that area a second coat. Cut off the braided mono about 2 feet from the end of the fly line and thread the end of it through the eye of a rugged craft needle (they make needles for just this purpose). Stick the point of the needle through the wall of the braid, about 4 inches back from the end, and run it through the hollow core of the braid for about 2 inches. Stick the needle through the side of the braid and pull it out,

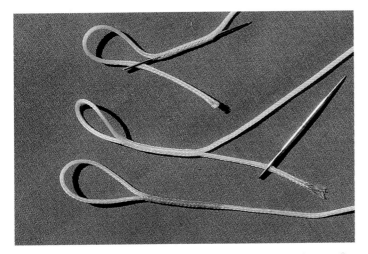

Figure 29   Braided mono loop. Thread the braid end through a needle. Push the needle into the fly-line core, run the needle up the hollow center for two inches, then push out through the wall. Pull the needle and braid end through with a pair of pliers. Coat junction with a Pliobond.

unthreading the braided mono from the eye as you go; this should leave about 2 inches of braided mono inside the hollow core. Pliobond the overlapped area. You should now have a 2-foot butt leader of braided mono with a 1-inch loop in the end to attach your leaders to.

I am also experimenting with using a similar but larger braided-mono loop on the end of my backing. So far it looks great (Fig. 30). Make the same loop, only longer, and thread your backing (using a needle) a couple of inches into the tag end of the braid, then out through the side. Tie a careful nail knot (see page 53) over the braid with the backing and coat the knot and the braid leading to the backing with Pliobond. After the Pliobond dries trim any errant fibers of braid and recoat the junction of the braid and backing until they become a smooth, rubbery oneness. The benefit I see here is that the braid will meet loop to loop with the braid at the end of your line; this will eliminate any possibility of one loop sawing through the other.

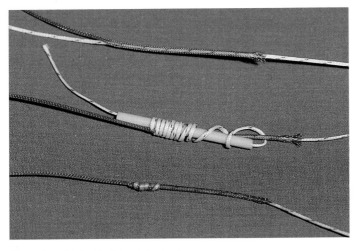

Figure 30   Joining backing to braided mono.

Beach Leaders

Tie a 1-inch-long double surgeon's loop in the end of a 3-foot piece of 30-pound-test mono. Now use a double surgeon's knot to join the other end to a 2-foot piece of 20-pound test, and tie a small double surgeon's loop in the end of the 20-pound. For tippets, tie small spider hitch (or Bimini twist) loops in 2-foot sections of 12-, 15-, and 20-pound-test monofilament. Loop-to-loop the 30-pound-test leader loop to the butt leader, and the tippet of your choice (I use 15-pound for most beach fishing, 20 if big fish are about) to the loop in the 20-pound-test end. This should give you a 9-foot leader, when the butt leader is taken into consideration. I carry extra leaders and tippets in my bag.

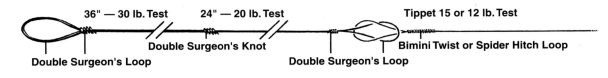

36" — 30 lb. Test   **24" — 20 lb. Test**   **Tippet 15 or 12 lb. Test**

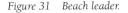

Double Surgeon's Knot

Double Surgeon's Loop   **Double Surgeon's Loop**   **Bimini Twist or Spider Hitch Loop**

Figure 31   *Beach leader.*

Boat Leaders

I actually use beach leaders in the boat to fish with small flies. For large flies and big fish I use the following formula: Tie a 1-foot-long spider hitch (or Bimini) in some 20-pound-test leader material. Do the same on the other end, so that you have 2 feet of 20-pound (not counting the knots) in between. Cut both loops in half. With a double surgeon's knot, tie a small double-line loop (just like in the backing, but much smaller, in one end). Connect the double line on the other end of the leader with a double surgeon's knot to a 2-foot section of 40-pound-test mono. This 40-pound serves as a shock or abrasion leader, and you can trim it to 10 inches if you want to be sure that you are IGFA (International Game Fish Association) legal. While I call this a "boat leader" because of the rough places and larger fish I pursue in the boat, don't hesitate to use it on a rocky beach if big fish are likely to be present. You don't need a heavy shock tippet to land big bass on a sand or mud bottom, but it can save the day if there are rocks around.

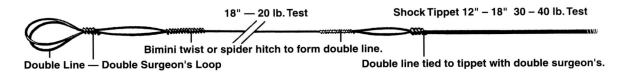

18" — 20 lb. Test   **Shock Tippet 12" – 18" 30 – 40 lb. Test**

Bimini twist or spider hitch to form double line.

Double Line — Double Surgeon's Loop   **Double line tied to tippet with double surgeon's.**

Figure 32   *Boat leader.*

These two leaders, beach and boat, will do the job. You may wish to tie your boat leader with lower-test lines all around for smaller fish, or your beach leader with 40-, 30-, and 20-pound-test tippets if you will be using a 10-weight on bigger fish. The formula is, however, the same, and all that you will need for any situation. It's important to mention that you don't need to tie leaders for either boat or beach. L.L. Bean offers both hand-tied and tapered (unknotted as in traditional freshwater fishing) leaders made especially for salt water. These are available in several tippet strengths, and a bite tippet can be added to them with a double surgeon's knot if you wish. These leaders will work just fine for striped bass fishing.

There are lots of good brands of mono out there, but be sure of their IGFA ratings if this is important to you. A line labeled 20-pound test can actually be 30-pound by IGFA standards. Fluorocarbons are also worth consideration. I find them to be brittle, and because of this knots don't pull down as smoothly. Unless you are very careful and lubricate the knot well, you will have poor knot strength. Lubricating the knot before pulling it tight reduces the heat that can severely weaken the line. Fluorocarbons are very abrasion resistant and very expensive. It's the hard finish of the fluorocarbon that makes it abrasion resistant; I've had some leaders of this material break after only a few fish, but a lot of casting. It may be that the more brittle nature of this material limits its longevity. Fluorocarbons are also said to be more resistant to the sun's ultraviolet rays, more transparent in the water, and less absorbent of water, which makes them stronger when wet. If you are very careful with your knots, a fluorocarbon leader might put a large fish in the boat that otherwise would have broken you off on a rock. I keep a number of boat leaders pretied and—whether mono or fluorocarbon—replace them at the slightest provocation. Every time I get into a hot school of stripers and get a little lazy about cutting back and retying my fly after every few bass, I end up breaking off a fish. It's best to be compulsive about fresh leaders and knots. Don't save leaders or leader material from one season to the next. The material becomes chalky and brittle, and the knot strength diminishes.

CHAPTER 6

Flies

As with baitfish, entire books have been written about saltwater fly designs. I love to tie flies, and I tie many patterns that are not going to appear here. While there may be some particular thing I like about a pattern that causes me to tie it and fish it, the five types of flies that I'll discuss below will arm you to the teeth for

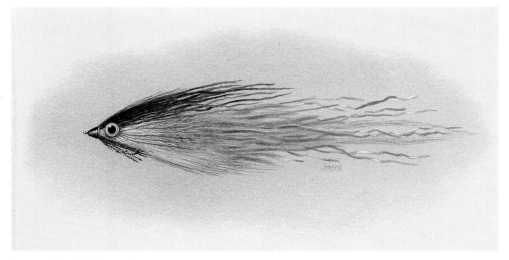

Figure 33   The Grocery fly.

your trips afield for stripers. This is not to say that many other flies don't work, because they do, and you may eventually want to buy or tie a far greater variety than I am going to mention. But you have to start somewhere, and you can walk into any situation with confidence if you're stocked up simply with these five flies in the variations, colors, lengths, and thicknesses that represent the important prey species where you'll be fishing.

The tying instructions included below are not necessarily identical to the original patterns. Sometimes the changes that I have made are for simplicity; sometimes for effectiveness.

The Lefty's Deceiver

You could successfully fish for not only stripers but also most of the world's fish with a selection of Deceivers—and this pattern is easily tied by the average fly tyer. (If you are a beginner, you should first take a course and/or read a book about basic fly tying.) The Deceiver is very versatile, and through small modifications to the tying

Figure 34   A selection of Lefty's Deceivers.

technique it can become a foot-long bunker fly or an 8-inch herring imitator called the Groceries. In small sizes a Deceiver can imitate a spearing; sparsely tied, it makes an excellent sand eel. The Lefty's Deceiver was invented by fly-fishing legend Lefty Kreh. The term *Groceries* was coined by the former director of L.L.Bean's fly-fishing school, Brock Apfel, the best all-around fly fisherman I know.

How to Tie the Deceiver

Figure 35-1   Deceiver/Grocery tying sequence.   Step 1

1. Select the hook size that you want to use. I like #1 for small patterns, #1/0 or #2/0 to imitate your general-purpose baitfish, and #3/0 to #5/0 for Groceries or bunker flies. I tie my Deceivers and most of my saltwater flies with Danville Flymaster Plus, which is a strong 3/0 thread. Wrap the shank with thread, then wrap from two to six saddle hackles onto each side of the hook shank. Select hackles depending on the size and thickness that you want—longer and thicker move more water and imitate bigger baitfish. Now fasten one or two pieces of regular or saltwater (for bigger flies) Flashabou to each side, and trim it to a length that extends just a bit beyond the hackles. This technique allows the Flashabou strands to flutter like a tail. To make the fly tough, lightly coat the wraps with your favorite cement.

Figure 35-2   Step 2

2. (Leave out step 2 and go directly to step 3 to tie a regular Deceiver.) To make a thick, water-moving fly like the Groceries, tie a clump of bucktail on top of the shank, halfway from the hackle butts to the eye. For an even bigger fly you can place another of these clumps on top of the hackle butts. To gain the high profile of a menhaden, **high-tie**—wrap under as well as over—these clumps, so that they stand up straighter. The biggest difference between a standard Deceiver and the Groceries is that the Deceiver is almost tubular in head-on profile; this is perfect for small baits like spearing or sand eels. The Groceries uses high ties on top and has thin sides to attain the oval profile of

Figure 35-3   Step 3

the herring or bunker. An important tying trick to use when you want to precisely fasten clumps of bucktail is to first make a wrap around only the bucktail clump, then work the clump tightly down against the shank and wrap normally over it. This is called locking the bucktail, and it works just like putting a strap around a stack of lumber—making it tough for the individual pieces to pull out and keeping the hair from rolling around the hook shank. Run a dubbing needle wet with cement through the base of the clump to cement the threads of the wrap.

3. Tie a clump of hair to the top of the hook just behind the eye, being careful to leave enough room so you will not crowd the head as you finish the fly. Now do

Figure 35-4   Step 4

the same thing on the bottom. If the fly you are tying is a smaller, thinner one to mimic a bait like a sand eel, let the material on the top and bottom meet to form the sides. If you want a more substantial fly you will need to separately wrap a thin layer of hair onto each side.

4. Add a thin layer of peacock herl to the top of your fly. This adds an olive sheen to the back that is shared by many baitfish. Tie a few strands of red Krystal Flash under the fly as gills, then spread a few strands of pearl Flashabou on each side of the fly and tie them in. Trim the flash

Figure 35-5   Step 5

materials on the side to just beyond the hook bend so that they will not wrap around the hook, and trim the gills to just in front of the hook point for the same reason.

5. Glue all the wraps, finish the head with 6/0 thread, and coat with five-minute epoxy or head cement. Attach an appropriately large stick-on eye to each side with a dab of Goop and you are finished.

Extras

To make a bunker fly, tie the same as for the Groceries, but first add a modest hank of Big Fly Fiber to the hook shank, just forward of the bend, before step 1. To tie a really large bunker fly, I make one high tie right in front of the last one, all the way to the head. You must keep each

Figure 36   A selection of Grocery flies.

individual tie sparse, however, or Mr. Universe couldn't cast the thing with a 14-weight. To help the fly sink quickly, wrap the shank—after the feathers are attached—from just in back of where the head will go back to the bend and forward

Figure 37   A selection of bunker flies.

again, if desired, with lead wire. I'm not big on weighting these flies since it's hard to get enough on to affect their sinking rate, and it makes the flies much harder to cast. Follow the colors described under "herring" and "bunker" in chapter 3 (Fig. 37).

The Clouser Minnow

Bob Clouser, a well-known smallmouth bass fisherman, invented the Clouser Minnow. As with the Deceiver, there have been many variations on the original design. It's a great fish catcher because it combines the wonderfully simple breathability of bucktail with a pair of lead dumbbell eyes. The eyes make the fly move up and down in the water column like a struggling baitfish. In the shallows, the fly can sink clear to the bottom and mimic a small flounder or crab. The fly is best kept in smaller sizes, especially because of the weighted eyes. The thin head doesn't move water the way a thicker, larger bait imitator like the Groceries will do.

How to Tie the Clouser Minnow

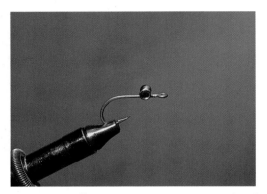

Figure 38-1   Clouser Minnow tying sequence.   Step 1

Figure 38-2   Step 2

Figure 38-3   Step 3

1. Choose a hook between #2 and #2/0, depending on the size of the fly desired, and place it in your vise. Wrap the thread (6/0 for below #1/0 hooks, and 3/0 for above) from the eye back down the shank to about a third of the way to the bend. Build up the threads in a $\frac{1}{2}$-inch area in the middle of the wrapped area and then, using X-, or figure-8-type wraps, secure a pair of appropriate-size dumbbell or bead-chain eyes (there are many types on the market; I like the ones onto which you can glue a stick-on eye) onto the bottom of the hook shank, so that the point will ride up and not snag on the bottom. Glue the wraps thoroughly and let the glue sink in, so that the eyes won't shift later.

2. On the same side of the hook as the eyes, wrap on a small clump of bucktail; if you are going to use any white, put it on first, since it will face down to the bottom. Secure the bucktail by wrapping near the eye. To get the bucktail to lie down, however, you will need to place a few wraps on the hook-bend side of the eyes. Don't make these wraps too tight or the bucktail will flare. Bring the thread back to the head.

Figure 39   A selection of Clouser flies.

3. Turn the hook over in the vise. At the head, tie in any flash material that you want (I like Krystal Flash). Now tie in your final clump of bucktail (often this is a darker color, as in a natural fish's coloration). Finish the head and apply cement. That was easy, wasn't it? Actually, of all the flies I'm showing you, only the Deceiver requires any real experience to tie.

Extras

You can make this fly longer by wrapping down the shank and tying in material at the end. I make some extended, heavily tied Clousers with monster eyes just for rip fishing (Fig. 39).

The Juve

Captain Pat Keliher came up with this basic concept as well as the name *Juve,* which is short for juvenile. As Pat ties this fly, it is a killer when schoolie bass are feeding on young herring. In many ways it shares the utter simplicity of the Clouser Minnow, but without the lead eyes—it uses large stick-on eyes instead, to duplicate the oversize eyes found on small herring. I have used this fly very successfully on nearly all the New England saltwater gamefish.

How to Tie the Juve

1. The Juve is meant to imitate small baitfish; a #1/0 hook is as big as necessary. To imitate bay anchovies or spearing, a #1 or #2 is sufficient. Use 6/0 thread. Captain Big Fish, as I named him during his full-time guiding days on Maine's Kennebec River, wrapped a little white bucktail on the bottom of the shank near the eye of the hook, and a little blue or green bucktail on the top. He then spread the two 180 degrees from each other, Gooped on a couple of eyes, and, in his thick Maine accent, "called it good." When the glue dries and the fly is placed in the water, the hair streams thinly back from the eyes, separated by the hook shank that serves as the lateral line.

Figure 40-1   Juvenile tying sequence.   Step 1

In my version, I substitute craft fur for bucktail, and add a little Lite Brite or Krystal Flash in the middle to provide shiny sides. Either material will work. I use the fur because it is much tougher, very supple in its action, and has a more appropriate, shorter length. It also is a good deal less expensive. I now tie most of my Juves with the material pulled back more

Figure 40-2   Step 2

straightly along the hook shank. I smooth the fibers parallel to the hook shank before I Goop on the eyes, which gives me a more natural profile.

Extras

You can wrap the shank of this hook with a piece of Flashabou, or paint the glue between the eyes with sparkle craft paints, but don't bother—it won't make this great fly any better than it is already (Fig. 41).

Here's a little story that speaks to this fly's caliber. During the 1997 season I was among 20 or so anglers waiting late one October afternoon at Lobsterville Beach, on

Figure 41   A selection of Juvenile flies.

Martha's Vineyard. Just before dusk a small school of false albacore blitzed along the beach, and everyone cast in turn as the fish passed by. Using a Juve—olive on top, white on the bottom, with some chrome Lite Brite in the middle—I caught the only fish. A half hour later the albacore came back and I missed a solid take; again, it was the only strike on the beach. I was very lucky, no question, and it could have all been sheer coincidence, but I'm glad I had the Juve on my line.

The Fur-Strip Fly

I wouldn't know who to credit for this one. Fur strips have been around as a tying material for a long time. They are incredibly versatile and full of action. Sometimes fur-strip flies that have been used in salt water become brittle after drying; if so, try to wet your fly for a few minutes before fishing it. It must be something to do with the tanning process, because they don't all seem to become stiff.

How to Tie Some Fur-Strip Flies

Style #1 (Fig. 42)

1. Sand eel or marine worm patterns are easy to tie with fur-strips. On a length of fur strip, measure the amount that you want hanging in back of the hook to imitate the baitfish's body. Notice how the fur naturally lies in one direction; tie your fur-strip so that, when it's retrieved, the water flows *with* this natural direction, not against it. With a dubbing needle separate the hairs down to the hide at that point, and cut the strip. Using 6/0 thread, simply bind the strip, fur-side up, to the area just in front of the bend on a hook that is proportioned to the length of the fur strip (bigger than #2/0 is unnecessary). Add a drop of glue to the wraps, being careful not to get it on the fur. Be careful, too, to cut between the hairs; don't cut off any hairs when you cut a fur strip. This embarrassingly simple fly can be cut later to the exact size you need to imitate small baitfish or worms.

Figure 42   Fur-strip—style 1.

Style #2 (Fig. 43)

1. Tie a few wraps of thread in a spot near the bend of the hook and glue them; do not cut the thread. With a dubbing needle, separate the fur at a distance from the end that leaves the length of tail you want. Bind the strip to the hook at the place where you separated the hairs, just forward of the bend, then wrap the shank of the hook forward to the head. Attach a set of lead eyes, if you wish, as in the Clouser instructions (see page 69).

Figure 43-1   Fur-strip—style 2.   Step 1

2. Palmer-wind the remainder of the fur strip up to the eye of the hook, then separate the fur and bind it to the hook. Trim off the excess, finish off the head, and glue the wraps. The body of fur on this style will fluff up and undulate in the water, creating great action.

Figure 43-2   Step 2

Extras

These simple patterns are effective imitations of all kinds of baitfish that have a wiggle action. You can add flash if you want by simply tying it in near the head or bend.

I like to use Lite Brite because it flows nicely along the fur. To make a great crab pattern, simply cut the fur off the top of the lead-eyed fly (make sure that you know which side will ride up). Keep the tail stubby and make a shell on top with a little silicone or sparkle craft paint.

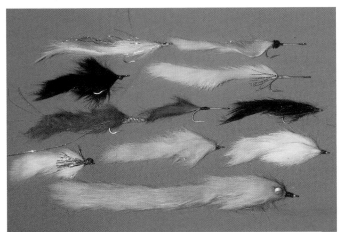

Figure 44   A selection of fur-strip flies.

I have taken some large bass in slow-moving water by slowly crawling a 10-inch fur-strip pattern, tied with ¼-ounce dumbbell eyes and fished on the end of a heavy sinking head. The secret was that the fly would wiggle enticingly even at retrieve speed of almost 0. This is probably as close as you can come to duplicating an eel—something a bass seldom will refuse. To tie a big fur-strip fly (bottom fly, Fig. 44), you must use a razor blade to cut your own custom strips from a whole rabbit skin.

Floating Flies

Years ago I was fishing Lobsterville Beach in the middle of a warm summer night, standing in a sparse line of other fly fishermen. Bass were popping here and there and had been for hours, though I had taken none. Every few minutes the guy to my right would make a groan, indicating a missed fish, or a faint *all right* followed by the screeching of his reel as a bass headed for deeper water. His scuffle with one fish took him past me to my left, as his bass swam with the current. When he returned he came close by me and I complimented him on his fish, hoping to draw him into a conversation. A friendly sort, as most striper fly rodders are, he turned his light on the fly in his hand. A #1/0 hook was encased in an inch-long black-colored cylinder of a material called Live Body. A very few pieces of black bucktail stuck out beyond the end along with two strands of Krystal Flash. The bass, he explained to me, were taking spearing from the surface. They didn't want the ones that were moving, he theorized; instead they were waiting under the spearing resting on the surface, picking out the vulnerable ones and taking them. The secret, he said, was no retrieve at all, just a dead drift. Since that night, his pattern and technique have helped me catch a lot of finicky stripers.

The Live Body Floater can be tied in the various thicknesses that the material comes in. In the thicker sizes it can be used as a popper. You can also use ostrich herl to give the fly an extended tail for use as a surface swimmer. There are other tubular or preshaped floating materials available, too, which you can also use to tie this fly.

How to Tie the Live Body Floater

1. Select a hook size between #2 and #2/0, depending on the diameter of Live Body you want to use. Make sure that your combination of hook and Live Body will float. A long-shanked hook isn't necessary. Wrap the shank of the hook with 6/0 thread. Near the bend of the hook, tie in some bucktail or marabou strands and a few pieces of Krystal Flash. Keep the number of wraps to a minimum. Use dark colors for night work, and light for daytime. The

length of the materials depends on how long you want your fly to be. One-half to one full length of the hook shank is about right. Keep the amount of materials fairly sparse.

2. With a razor, cut a piece of Live Body or select a preshaped body. I most frequently use a size about the diameter of a pencil, and a length that will reach from the hook eye to the bend. Heat a dubbing needle until it glows, and then, rotating both the Live Body and the needle as you go, slide and melt your way through the length of the cylinder. The rotation will help you stay in the center.

3. Coat the wraps on your hook with a thin layer of five-minute epoxy, and insert the eye of the hook into the hole through the Live Body. Clean off any excess epoxy while it dries with a dubbing needle. Be careful not to squeeze epoxy onto your tail materials.

Extras

You can color these flies with markers, or apply glitter to a light coat of epoxy. Eyes can be Gooped on the flies—although for night fishing I wouldn't bother. This fly, like the others, is tough and versatile. In various sizes and colors it will fill the need for almost any floating fly (Fig. 46).

Figure 45-1   Floating fly tying sequence.   Step 1

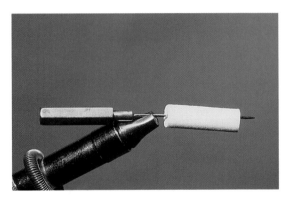

Figure 45-2   Step 2

Figure 45-3   Step 3

Figure 46   A selection of floating flies.

Other Flies

Figure 47   Other effective flies for striper fishing: 1. black sand eel with marabou collar and braided head, 2. Popovics's 3D, 3. Fly Fur sand eel with epoxy head, 4. Fly Fur herring, 5. braided tubing sand eel, 6. Surface Slider, 7. epoxy herring with Fly Fur tail, 8. black braided tubing sand eel, 9. light bunker fly tied with Icelandic sheep hair.

CHAPTER 7

Clothing
and Accessories

Boat Fishing

The correct clothing is as important to a successful fishing trip as the selection of equipment. It seems that even in the best days of summer, if I simply jump aboard and head out, I invariably wish that I had put just a few more minutes into organizing and brought along something I'd forgotten. Here, then, is a compilation of the things I find important on the typical boat-fishing trip for stripers.

Let's start with the feet. If I wear sneakers or boat shoes, at some time during the day I manage to get my feet wet. This often happens as I'm putting gear in or launching the boat. At best, my feet end up wet with dew. I thus wear a pair of short boots in the boat and carry a pair of sneakers in a waterproof gear bag. Seldom do I end up putting on the sneakers.

I also start the day wearing breathable foul-weather pants and top. Again, I find that at running speed, and what with morning dew, spray, and cool ocean air, I often leave this waterproof clothing on all day to stay dry and to keep the wind chill down. If you are going out to buy a set, I suggest that you get pants that have no buckles or straps that might snag your line; get a jacket that hangs down well below your waist, too, to keep your middle warm and dry. I very much like elastic cuffs and ankles since they keep water out and provide no ends for fly lines to catch on. You might as well get a jacket made for fishing that has some nice big pockets and a hood. You simply cannot beat a hood for warmth, and if you draw it up snugly, it will also keep you comfortable on a long run in an open boat.

Except in the summer, I like to wear fleece—fleece pants, fleece top (preferably with a hood), and microfleece undergarments. This clothing is warm, light, and flexible, and it dries very quickly. In cool, windy weather, you can't beat Windstopper or Windbloc fleece, especially if worn under foul-weather gear. One piece of cold-weather clothing that I've come to love is a fleece neck gaiter. When under way in a boat it's a real luxury. If I need to strip down later in the day, I put the layers into the waterproof bag that my sneakers go in (Fig. 49).

I have a difficult time wearing warm gloves when fishing. I've tried different kinds of fingerless gloves, and find the fleece type a bit slimmer in the palm, which lets me better hold on to the rod. Except in the coldest conditions, I get by just wearing wool gloves between fishing spots. In

Figure 48   The beauty of modern materials such as Gore-Tex and fleece is that clothing made from them can come on and off easily in layers. A waterproof hat brim under a foul-weather hood keeps the hood from covering your eyes.

warmer weather I find that my fly lines dry out and stick to my fingers during my retrieve. L.L. Bean sells a stripping glove with a leather-driving-glove-type palm and Lycra half fingers, however, that has been wonderful for me. My hands don't get sore, and the line slips easily through my fingers on the retrieve or when fighting a fish. In warm, sunny weather these sun gloves, especially with some hand moisturizer underneath, also help keep my hands from burning or drying out (Fig. 50).

In rainy weather I wear a baseball hat under my hood. The stiff visor holds the hood out from my face, and the hat is reasonably aerodynamic—but cold. I've thus got a Windbloc fleece hat with earflaps that I wear when it's cold. Even though the visor flops up and down when I'm under way, it's still the best cool-weather hat that I've found.

Exposure is always an issue when fishing from a boat along the northern half of the East Coast. The weather is typically much cooler in the morning and evening than at midday. During the height of the day—typically the worst time for stripers anyway—you may need to deal with hot weather and intense glare from the sun. Much has been learned of late about the sun's effects on skin, including the identification

Figure 49   Bags like this L.L. Bean Kennebecker keeps clothing and equipment dry while on the water.

of UVB as the most harmful ray. Materials like Solarweave, which L.L. Bean uses in a line of clothing called SPF Tropic Wear, block up to 99 percent of harmful UV rays. I don't want a lot of sun exposure, so I wear full-length pants, socks, and a long-sleeved shirt. I use plenty of sunblock but generally do not wear the flats-type hats, simply because they're hot and tend to blow off my head. They probably aren't a bad idea, however, if you're comfortable with them.

Glasses of some kind should always be worn when fly fishing, if only for the eye protection. An optometrist friend of mine tells me that clear plastic lenses block out much of the sun's UV rays. Ideally you need two pair of glasses for striped bass fishing. Photochromic sunglasses provide the best daytime-fishing protection. These glasses block out 100 percent of UV rays and, because they lighten or darken depending on conditions, give you optimum flexibility between seeing through surface glare on sunny days and retaining normal visibility when it's cloudy. For night fishing or dusk or dawn

Figure 50   Three fly-fishing gloves, left to right: fingerless fleece, sun gloves, and neoprene for the coldest weather.

work, you still want maximum light availability, and that means clear lenses. I've found amber superior to green for looking into the water, although there are different lens colors (including variations of amber) that serve different purposes. Side shields reduce glare and offer additional protection. The experts who staff the L.L. Bean Fly-Fishing Hotline are trained to advise people on the various options the company offers (see page 41 for the number).

Since I fish from three different small powerboats, I want my tackle stored so that it can be easily moved from garage to car, boat, and back. My solution has been to have one large tackle bag (preferably waterproof) that holds all of my boat-fishing gear (Fig. 51). Other than flies, the inventory includes: pliers (I like long nosed), a file, spare lines held on Rio spools, a plastic bag full of paper towels, a flashlight, line dressing, a knife capable of cutting rope, a leader wallet, a handheld VHF, a handheld GPS, binoculars, a plastic bag to bring home a fish, and a cellular phone. I often bring a night scope to help me navigate before daybreak. I keep safety gear stored on the boat—and I'll discuss that, along with rod storage, in chapter 8. I also have a pair of line nippers, on a clip-on retractor, fastened to the outside of the bag. I've found that, other than food and water, this list does the job for me.

When boat fishing for stripers, I keep all of my flies in large plastic boxes that fit into my bag. Because I do a lot of prospecting for large fish, I have one box just for Groceries and bunker flies in various colors. A second box houses Deceivers and Clousers; fur-strips and Juves are in a third. Floating flies, along with my small epoxies for bonito, go into a fourth. Each box is clearly labeled with a waterproof marker and stored in my bag so that I can read the labels when I open the flap. I love to tie, and am constantly trying to improve my patterns. I put all of my new

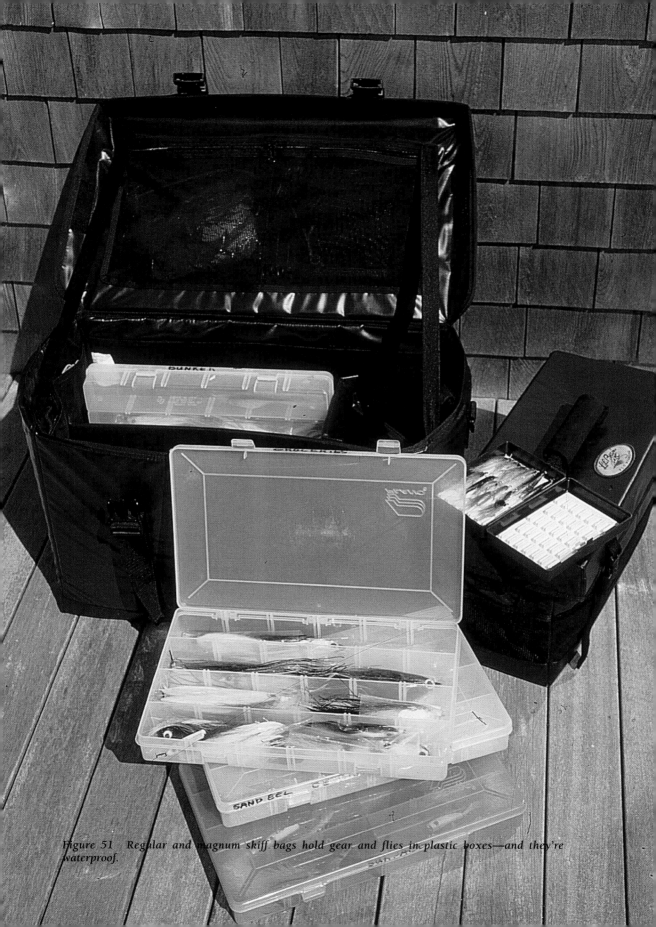

Figure 51   Regular and magnum skiff bags hold gear and flies in plastic boxes—and they're waterproof.

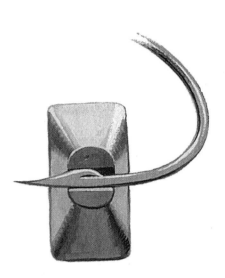

Figure 52   *Debarbing a hook.*

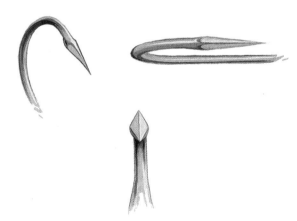

Figure 53   *A sharpened hook.*

flies into plastic sleeves to keep them separate; it's pleasurable and confidence building to take a new fly I'm enthusiastic about and start fishing with it. It's after each day's use that I fall down in my fly maintenance. What I should all do is wash my flies in fresh water after use, and let them air-dry before storage. Maybe I'll start next season.

Fly hooks, whether for boat or shore use, can't be kept sharp enough. Mash down the barbs (Fig. 52), too—the hooks will penetrate better if you do, and with the "conservation bend" that I'll discuss in the final chapter (see page 200), you'll land just as many fish. Sharpen the hooks by filing them to a long point on the outside of the bend (Fig. 53). If you sharpen the inside, the edge will cut but not stick. Sharpening the outside will allow your hook to pass the **fingernail test**—will the hook catch readily as you slide it along the outside of your fingernail? It should, if you want maximum hookups (Fig. 54). If your hook rusts, break off the point to make a practice fly; a rusty hook may give out during a fight.

Figure 54   *To test the sharpness of a hook.*

Shore Fishing

Striped bass fishing can find you wading over diverse shorelines. Mud flats, rocky shores, jetties, sod banks, shallows, sand beaches, and steep ocean sand beaches are all important striper places. A lot of this fishing doesn't require waders; if the shoreline is steep and the waves small, you may do very little wading. My shore fishing on the south side of Cape Cod has me hopping from jetty to jetty and walking marsh banks, but not real wading. I'm also in and out of the car and reaching for keys all day, so I frequently dress just as I suggested for boat fishing: in foul-weather gear and a pair of calf-high boots. I also, however, do a lot of fishing that requires waders.

For wading in gentle waters I like stocking-foot waders. I have a pair of breathable stocking-foot waders that I wear with a pair of neoprene booties. This setup is easy to deal with and as comfortable as pants. The one problem with stocking feet on a sand beach is that sand can get between your waders and your boot. In a short while the sand can build up enough to drive your foot out.

On sand beaches and for easy on and off, you can't beat boot-foot waders. If you are heading into a November ocean for six hours, go with neoprene; most of the time, however, a regular insulated pair of waders is fine. I like to wear fleece pants or undergarments under my waders, and heavier fleece pants if it's cold. If your suspenders tend to fall off your shoulders, try crossing them in front; this has worked well for me for years. A wading belt will keep water out of your waders should you step in too deeply,

and it's an important safety option; always wear one over your waders. I usually wear mine over my wading jacket for additional protection. Buy only nonslip soles, like felt or L.L. Bean's Aqua Stealth. I wear them on sand, too, with no problem (Fig. 55).

As far as the rest of your clothing is concerned, I see your needs as similar to those in boat fishing. I even prefer a

Figure 55   Olive/brown Aqua Stealth boots by L.L. Bean. (Photo by L.L. Bean)

regular-length wading jacket, since it keeps me warmer by placing another layer around my waist. Just remember that if you hurry along and work up a sweat you will either stay hot, or freeze. This is where Gore-Tex and other breathable materials, either for jackets or waders, can make your life more comfortable. I try to be leisurely on the beach, especially if I'm going to be there for hours. Besides, you can be seriously hurt by hurrying over rocks.

Your shore-fishing equipment needs, however, differ from those of boat fishing. The first big difference is your inability to carry a lot of gear with you. Shore fishing means you have to travel light. This isn't really much of an issue, since you'll only have one weight of rod with you, and you won't have the variety of conditions to face that you might in a boat. But what should you use to carry your gear? The two large pockets on the front of many wading jackets may be sufficient for a short outing. I've often gone wade fishing with a couple of fly wallets, a pair of pliers, a file, and a few tippets stuffed into my jacket pockets. I do like, however, to carry a few extra flies, in case I run into different bass-feeding situations. I also typically put a camera in one jacket pocket; a case for my glasses and a bag of paper towels in the other.

At the beginning of the season I stuff five wallets and one box of flies, leaders, tippets, pliers, file, a Ziploc bag containing a pad impregnated with line dressing, a spare flashlight, and a tube of bug spray into a large **chest pack** (a gear bag worn against the chest) (Fig. 56). During the season I restock this bag as needed, and I simply grab it every time I head for the beach. The bag also has a Velcro holder for my pliers on one end, and tall, thin pockets on the other that hold files, bug dope, and a spare flashlight. While the flies I carry are similar to those I stock for boat fishing, I don't have any really big ones, and I carry only a couple of smaller Groceries. Instead I have many more thin, small flies to imitate the sand eels, grass shrimp, spearing, and immature fish like small herring that I expect to find along the shoreline. I like fly wallets for carrying a limited quantity of thin streamers. They're easy to open (I don't bother to zip or fasten them) and all of my flies are immediately visible. The whole setup is very compact and convenient. You will, however, need a box to deal with your poppers, which don't store well in a wallet.

Figure 56   A chest pack is handy for carrying a fair amount of gear when wading.

An alternative to a chest pack is a **wading vest.** These come in various lengths, material types, and capacities (with more or fewer pockets and gear-holding options). Vests are an especially good option if you want to carry some extra gear. I wear a pair of nippers on a retractor; these are indispensable to me. Stay away from an external fly patch in the salt. You'll either pull the thing apart or lose your flies. L.L. Bean has developed a good alternative on its better vests called the Fly-of-the-Day Pocket, which features a quick-open (and -close), Velcro-fastened, expandable pocket that houses a foam fly patch. If a fly falls off it simply lands in the pocket so it's not lost. The quick accessibility to a few hot flies that the external patch offers is retained without the patch's drawbacks.

There are a few pieces of safety equipment that you'd be wise to take out on the beach. At night you will need a light. Some of the new high-tech lights are light, bright, and have terrific battery life. I always carry two. I often wear them both around my neck, and I'll turn them both on when climbing down a jetty—one in my teeth so I can aim it, and one hanging straight down to illuminate the general area. A handheld cellular phone is also a very good idea. Not only does it offer the obvious safety considerations, but if your fishing partner is also carrying a cellular, or if you both are carrying handheld VHFs, you can simultaneously search separate fishing areas—doubling your chances of running into fish. Inflatable suspenders provide extra safety both in the surf and on the boat. And believe it or not, a compass can be important on some beaches. Even though I had fished Popham Beach's Morse River outlet for years, for instance, there came one summer night "thick a dungeon of fog"—as they say in Maine—on the 1/2-mile-long sand flat that goes out at low tide when I became completely turned around. The foghorn on Seguin seemed to be blowing from all directions; meanwhile, the tide was creeping into the twisted channel between me and the high beach. I got a bit nervous before I stumbled into the surf line, and I kept that noise at my back until I hit high ground. People have fared worse, though. A small pocket compass is a good idea.

One other essential piece of beach-fishing equipment is a **stripping basket** (Fig. 57). Line stripped in without a basket will become tangled around your legs because of the in-and-out action of the waves. It will also become covered with sand, abrading your rod guides and destroying the line itself. There are basically two types of baskets on the market—one made largely of mesh material, the other essentially a dishpan. In fact, my first stripping basket (which after 10 years I have no problem with) came to me in the Rubbermaid shipping box that the tackle company must have gotten it in. The company hooked a strap to it, stuck a few pieces of 200-pound-test mono in the

Figure 57   This angler demonstrates the use of a stripping basket. (Photo by Rob Bossi)

bottom to keep the loops from tangling, and drilled a couple of holes in it so that it would drain. The only problem with this design is that it's totally opaque, so you can't see where you're walking, especially not at night. Some of the mesh baskets lose their shape, however, and they're certainly not as durable as the rubber dishpan. Still, whichever design you choose, you need one. Do get the kind that has something in the bottom to keep the loops from tangling. When I'm fishing for schoolies from a rocky shore, I quickly lift these baby bass into the basket, where I unhook them. This keeps them from falling to the rocks if they slip out of my hands. Don't adjust your basket so tight that you cannot swivel it around your waist to your hip if you need to bend over; to drop to your knees in the sand, to work on a larger fish you have beached; or to see your footing by flashlight.

Besides holding my line, I find a basket to be a great place to rest my hands while I perform two-handed strips; to facilitate this, I wear my basket a bit higher than most other fly casters (see page 101). This also helps me wade a little deeper. And here's a tip that will save you some grief: After you start to retrieve the fly, reach into your basket and toss out the first few feet of recovered line. This will give you enough slack that your casting movement will not tangle the line in the bottom of your basket on the next cast.

C H A P T E R   8

Boats

Small Boats

I've fished for stripers from nearly everything that floats, except perhaps a float tube. (I've seen plenty of people use float tubes, though, and if you are confident of the waters that you're in, I'm sure they can be fun and effective.) Stripers are creatures of near-shore waters, and in many places they can be fished for from a tiny craft. On any body of water connected to the ocean, however, for your own safety you should understand what the worst-case scenario might be and prepare yourself for it. Let's say you take your canoe to fish a coastal river. You discover a school of fish at high tide in a sheltered cove. As the tide drops, you follow the feeding fish out into the channel, and before you know it the 3-knot tides sweep you downriver. Later you decide to head back upriver—only to find that what was a point of land when you passed it coming down is now a tumbling tide rip, complete with whirlpools you don't dare cross. You're faced with several unhappy choices. If you had stayed in the cove and pulled out as the tide dropped, you would've been fine. And that's exactly what you should have done. On the other hand, a 14-foot aluminum boat with a small electric motor, in addition to the 10-horsepower main engine, draws only an inch or two more water and could've easily brought you home.

Figure 58   The Old Town Discovery boat is as light as a canoe but rowable. Note how the skiff bag, rod-on-reel case, red Kennebecker gear bag, and life preserver all fit nicely inside.

I keep an Old Town Discovery Sport Boat on the salt pond in front of my Cape Cod house (Fig. 58). The pond is shallow and protected, and I never take the boat through the inlet to Vineyard Sound. I need a boat that I can easily drag up the path to the shore, and I love the peacefulness of rowing it around. However, a small aluminum boat that I could stand up in would be a better fishing platform in every respect.

If you are not experienced with navigating the salt, seek out a friend who can help you peruse a chart that covers your intended trip before you venture onto the water. Never venture onto tidal water without a chart. If everything you plan is clearly within the capabilities of you and your craft, fine. But remember that there is no bargaining with the ocean; no turning back the clock if you find you've bitten off more than you can chew. Leaving a note at home that includes your trip plan is a good idea whether you're boat or shore fishing.

If you are going to acquire a small boat for inshore striper fishing, I cannot recommend highly enough a good-quality, relatively high-sided, aluminum boat of at least 14 feet (Fig. 59). I've spent thousands of hours in such craft, and taken bass of all sizes from them. With a small electric winch, even an angler with a bad back can trailer one. They are frugal on fuel, yet can really make time. A 14-foot-deep fisherman type can practically run on wet mud, yet it still allows you to stand and move around without fear of capsizing. When you start boating the coast you'll likely find yourself attracted to the tide rips and surf lines just outside the protected waters of the estuaries. A midteen-size aluminum boat can take you there in safety—on bluebird days. With a little experience and a cool head on your part, it will probably bring you back even if you make a mistake about the conditions, although you won't enjoy the trip one bit. Nonetheless, this aluminum boat is probably your most sensible entry point to inshore fly fishing for stripers. Don't compromise by getting a smaller craft; the smaller craft makes virtually all of the compromises.

Figure 59   An 18-foot aluminum boat modified with a raised deck, extended tiller, and grab rail for stability. Note that the throw life ring is always a good thing to have aboard.

I have a few thoughts on outfitting and fishing from a 14- to 16-foot "tin boat." Keep it simple. Everything that you attach to your boat can catch fly lines. On motors of over 15 horsepower, an electric start is nice, so you'll probably have a battery—which allows you to run a depth sounder as well. You can use a portable depth recorder, but the kind that runs from a 12-volt battery is better. Having played with both, I also like the permanently mounted transducer. Don't be afraid to buy the simplest recorder; all of these machines have more features than you need. I almost never take mine off automatic. A flat floor is nice, but unless it is factory installed I bet it will catch your fly line. Since wiring doesn't last long around salt water, use portable, battery-powered running lights.

While it can be done, I wouldn't bother trying to build comprehensive rod storage into a boat. The rod-on-reel storage I suggested earlier (see page 82) is fine, and allows you to make a smooth transition to and from your craft. I'd stay away from consoles and windshields on a small boat—they will just be in the way. Also, the farther forward you sit in these boats, the harsher your ride becomes. A padded helmsman's

Figure 60   These anglers used "tin" boats to reach an otherwise inaccessible marshy shoreline where they took this nice bass while wading. (Photo by Pip Winslow).

seat with a back support is a great idea, even if you have to mount it on top of an existing cross seat. A folding back-support seat for your friends will make their days a lot more comfortable. There are lots of adjustable-fabric types on the market.

I'm a fan of electric motors. Later I'll discuss a special bow-mounted setup (see page 97), but you need a stern one also. I guess if I could only have one motor, I'd choose a transom mount. Use it to correct a drift in shallow water, to inch along a shoreline, to sneak up on breaking fish, and, if need be, as an emergency power source. If you're going to do any sight fishing, you'll probably need a pole. I say "probably" because the bow-mounted electric motor setup below can, to a large degree, replace it. You can spend a lot of money on a good Florida-style glass or graphite pole, but if you're serious about flats fishing for stripers, you should get one. Another way to start is with a telescoping aluminum pole that includes a device called a **duck's foot,** which spreads out to offer resistance when pushed into a soft bottom yet collapses to a small diameter so that you can easily pull it out. If you stand on the seats of a 14- to 16-foot aluminum boat you can see surprisingly well, and with a telescoping pole you can often pole yourself along from the rear seat.

Medium to Big Boats

If you want to fish many of the better pieces of big-bass water near you, consider a boat of between 17 and 20 feet. Many manufacturers offer excellent fly-fishing

Figure 61   You need a good boat to fish tide rips like this one trying to climb over Capt. Steve Bellefleur's stern. (Photo by Duncan Barnes)

boats in this size range. I set the upper size limit at around 20 feet because, having fished from many boats in this range, I know that some are too big for certain aspects of the job. Stripers are near-shore creatures, and the better fly-fishing spots often require you to drift between rocks—in which you must have a good feel for the location of both ends of your boat. Also, many spots are simply too shallow for a larger boat. That doesn't mean you can't fly fish for stripers in a 25-foot, deep-V cuddy-cabin boat. You can, and if your intention is to exclusively fish offshore tide rips, you may want one even larger. Still, if you have such a craft, then your boating sophistication is really beyond this discussion. My only advice for you would be to look out for rod storage, and to keep the boat as clean as possible, for the sake of your fly lines.

Figure 62   Note the fly-line-friendly setup of the author's boat: no superstructure, tubes for the rod tips, and a large open area to fish from. (Photo by Chip Bates)

How should you select and outfit the 17- to 20-foot boat? Here are some thoughts. First, for fly fishing you want a boat on which nothing sticks up in the air. Having to cast around a T-top, Bimini top, radar stanchion, or even walk-through windshield is difficult at best. Sooner or later you're going to stick a hook through a plastic window, or even break a rod. You should also avoid raised bow rails. I can guarantee that you'll smash your rod and/or reel into a high bow rail from time to time; it could also very well cause you to break a rod on a good fish.

Center consoles are fashionable these days, and they do give you a bit of dry storage, some protection from the elements, and something to hold on to. The drawbacks are that they chew up a lot of room, that small boats ride a lot better aft than amidships, and that you have to get out from behind the console to cast. My 17-foot boat has tiller steering from a single pedestal seat located 2 feet in front of the transom (Fig. 63). My spartan complement of gauges and switches, as well as my depth finder, are all mounted in the combing at my side. Guests sit on a large dry-storage-box seat located two-thirds of the way forward. This gives both my guests and me a

Figure 63   The author's 17-foot boat set up for saltwater fly fishing for stripers—maximum space, minimum complexity. (Photo by the author)

large uncluttered area immediately in front of us that is perfect to fly cast from. When approaching breaking fish, the helmsman has only to step forward and cast—and sometimes the 15 seconds you save because you didn't have to climb out from behind the console is all the time you have before the fish go down. A number of manufacturers now offer this type of configuration, especially in aluminum, in boats of up to 20 feet. Mine has a fiberglass hull; I purchased a bare commercial hull, and a local boatyard did the outfitting.

No boat in this size range is going to ride as softly as you'd like. Still, if you get a boat with a sharp front entry and trim tabs, you can bring its bow down, which allows it to plane at lower speeds and to present a sharper entry to the waves. Even a nearly flat hull won't pound as hard if you don't push it out of the water. Also, look for a hull with good flare, so that you won't be soaked all the time.

Pick a hull that has a nonskid deck and a combing that comes up to at least the top of the shins of the bow caster. Not only do the sides give you something to lean against, to sit down on, and to contain you in rough standing conditions, but they also keep your line from blowing out of the boat.

You need rod storage under the gunwales so that you won't step on your rods, and ideally every rod should have a tube for its tip to slide into. Fly rods break very

Figure 64   A low freeboard, as on this boat, can easily send the angler over the side. (Photo by Harvey Wheeler)

easily, and 90 percent of the time the tip is the casualty. You'll need elastic cords or straps to keep the rods from sliding out, too. I once had a rod slide out of a factory rod holder in rough water. It slid backward and within 15 minutes the underside of the gunwales had sanded right through the blank.

A built-in fuel tank is a nice feature. My little 17-footer holds 40 gallons, and with a four-cycle outboard, I cannot use this much fuel even in three days of fishing. Besides, I have one less thing above decks, and the tank's weight is forward to help smooth out my ride.

Even if you have dockage you may want to trailer a 17- to 20-foot boat to take to other fishing areas. Get an electric winch (one size bigger than you think you need), then run a pull cord aft along the trailer frame and dead-end it. Once you hook the boat to your winch cable, you have only to pull on the cord from anywhere to activate

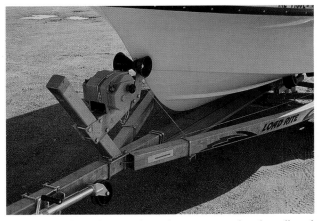

Figure 65   The author's trailer with a power winch—the pull cord runs to the end of the trailer—and a center walkway. (Photo by the author)

the winch. Build a walkway (I used a plank, along with some nonskid) to the back of your trailer so you can hook up your boat without getting wet. With a self-loading trailer set up like this, you can pull your boat onto the trailer alone even in a moderate wind.

The ocean can be a cold place, even in the summer. Always be prepared for an emergency. In addition to the required flares and whistle, you should have a medical kit and a space blanket. Other important safety equipment includes a marine radio, cellular phone, good compass, paddle, and anchor with enough line to provide a three-to-one anchoring scope in the deepest area you're likely to be in. I'd also like to make a big pitch that you carry a handheld GPS. I don't see a lot of inshore striper-fishing applications for the GPS, but offshore and combined with a compass—possibly a night scope—it greatly enhances your navigation ability.

The Bow-Mounted Electric Motor

A remote-control, bow-mounted electric motor is the single greatest fishing enhancement that you can add to most boats between 14 and 20 feet in length. I did tell you earlier that I'd choose a transom mount if I could have only one. And a transom mount can indeed be much more quickly deployed than a bow mount, without having to go to the bow to do so; it's also good for approaching a fishing location quietly, or quickly and quietly moving away from anything you've drifted too close to. The transom mount, however, requires constant attention to keep the steering on track; you can't fly cast and steer it at the same time. A remote-control bow-mounted unit, on the other hand, allows you to fly fish while it pulls you along your desired path.

Let's say that you want to work a stretch of deep, oceanfront beach. The boat glides to a stop 150 feet off the beach and you leave the outboard in the water, pointing dead ahead to keep the stern from excessive drift. After selecting a prospecting outfit—a 10-weight, 350-grain Superhead, and mullet-colored Groceries—you walk to the bow of the boat (so you can observe the direction indicator on top of the motor) and fold the electric motor forward into the water. The dessert-plate-size control panel, which is light enough to float, is positioned around your chest on a strap made from an old chest pack. You're familiar enough with the locations of the raised, knobby buttons of the control panel to use them at night. You turn the motor on and push the throttle button until the second indicator lights up on the motor's control panel. You note that the direction indicator is pointed straight down the beach but quickly sense that the boat is slowly moving toward the shore, due to the breeze. A little touch on the left-side directional button corrects for the breeze, and now you're moving slowly right down the beach, about 100 feet offshore. With both hands free, you cast into the white water and pull your fly toward the boat in moderate strips, keeping a constant eye on the boat's progress and correcting well in advance for an oncoming point of land. Then you hook a large bass at the end of the rip. As the fish peels off line, you turn the electric motor to pull the boat offshore, finally stopping the motor to fight and land the bass. After releasing a nice cow, you sit down to get your balance as the motor's maximum-thrust setting pulls you back up to the point for another pass. Some units can substitute a voice-command control for the push buttons; some let you enter a compass course, which the motor will then automatically steer the boat toward.

I spent one pleasant midday this past season fishing a flat with my 17-foot Parker. Standing on top of my storage-box seat, I enjoyed tremendous visibility as I moved along the edge of deeper water where bass were holding on a shallow sandy lip. With my remote control requiring only occasional correction, my hands were both free to cast to any fish I saw. The bass let me approach well within casting range before unhurriedly moving out of the boat's path.

There are still more benefits to this system: moving in and out around rocks, use of the momentary control to sneak up on feeding fish, or even turning the motor in a complete circle to back the boat away from a boulder. Properly installed and used to its best advantage, the remote-control electric will put a lot of extra bass in your boat.

PART III

Fishing Techniques and Know-How

C H A P T E R   9

Fly Casting
for Stripers

The basic principles of good technique are the same for all fly casting. A few special tips may, however, help you cast to striped bass. If you are a good caster already, you'll quickly grasp the terms and information that follow. If not, L.L. Bean offers in-depth instruction in basic and advanced fly casting. (For information, check out the L.L. Bean Fly-Fishing Catalog.)

First of all, a lot of your casting faults can be corrected with a single change: longer arm movements. This includes both your double-haul motion and the distance that you move your casting arm. Most anglers will have fewer tailing loops, tighter casting loops, and higher line speed—and will more easily pull the fly and end of the fly line from the water—if they fully extend their arms while casting. Just remember that your hand must go in a straight line from the end of your backcast to the end of your forward cast. There is a tendency for this hand to rise in the center of the stroke and fall on each end, forming a bit of an arc. This arc causes a wide loop, slows line speed, can cause tailing loops, and will definitely cause your fly to hit the beach or water behind you. But a straight-line movement, as if your hand were on a track, will efficiently deliver power to your line. Combine long, level arm movements with a stiff wrist and a double haul and you have most of the elements of distance casting.

Casting with the wind blowing onto your rod-hand side is dangerous. There are, however, a number of things you can do to facilitate fishing under these conditions. First, if the wind is strong, turn your back to it and make your backcast perpendicular to its direction. If the wind is moderate, use a water haul to touch your fly down in front of you for just a second; this will stop the fly and line from blowing to your left as you start your backcast. Also, try a sidearm motion to make your backcast. Between these two techniques, you can usually clear your body. Once you have worked out enough line you're ready for your final backcast. Angle this last backcast a bit higher into the air, and shoot out the rest of the line that you need to load your rod. Then, casting your rod on a near-vertical plane, allow your line to drift with the wind over your head as you send the fly forward.

For some time I have been working on casting with my left hand. I've not taken this as seriously as I'd like to, but I can do it passably, as long as distance isn't required. I recently spent an evening beach fishing with stripers at my feet and a stiff wind blowing down the beach toward my right side. It was pleasant to be able to fish these conditions comfortably by simply switching to my left hand.

Striped bass fishing, especially from boats, is most productive with lines like Superheads, which are relatively short and dense and therefore require little false casting. To cast these lines effectively don't false cast them in the air; the density of the heads make them hard to control. Instead touch your fly and the tip of your line onto the water and, in the same motion with which you finish your forward cast, start your backcast. The fly must just kiss the water. Continue this water-haul technique until you have worked out all of the head. The water haul must be one smooth motion; as my friend George Watson says, "If you wait one second too long, you're meat." On your last backcast shoot out a few feet of line, just enough that no part of the head will reenter the guides when you double haul. With a long, smooth rod motion, make your forward cast. At all costs avoid quick, short, jerky strokes of the rod, since the reciprocating weight of these lines will cause all kinds of problems. Tight loops and high line speeds are not needed or desired. The mass of these heads will carry your fly easily, even into the wind. Once mastered, this technique allows a good caster to retrieve the fly, make one roll cast and one water haul, then shoot an 80-foot cast in calm air. Very little time is wasted false casting compared to conventional lines.

Finally, try to cultivate the habit of forming a circle with the thumb and index finger of your line hand and letting the cast slip through that circle, rather than abandoning the line altogether while it is shooting. From time to time you may want to stop a cast short. If the water is shallow, you may want to instantly start a retrieve. More important, you may want to set the hook in a fish that grabs your fly the second it touches the water. Keeping your fingers in touch with the line is vital to performing all these maneuvers.

C H A P T E R   1 0

Feeding
Areas

In the fall of 1997, a friend of mine and I salvaged a blown-out day on the boat by fishing the east jetty on the Cape Cod Bay side of the canal. The wind gusted to well over 30 knots as we walked the jetty, but it was at our backs, making casting

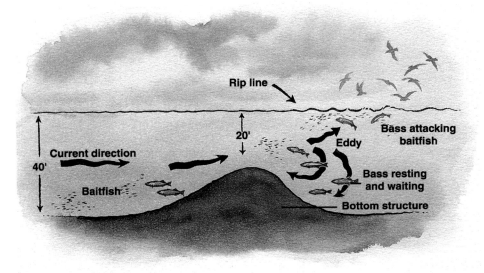

Figure 66   Submerged structure.

possible. We were told that a school of stripers had been on the surface an hour earlier but had gone down. Everyone was standing around idly, hoping for another bust.

We realized something, however, that the other anglers missed: About halfway to the end the current ran into the jetty, forming a seam that left the rocks at an angle and creating a back eddy on the downcurrent side. From the jetty out as far as we could cast, then, bass were stacked up along that seam. They greedily ate our flies. Our ability to find those fish was based on understanding the bass's feeding system.

There are several kinds of structure that bass find advantageous when feeding. All of these feeding stations do one essential thing: give the bass a physical advantage over the bait. In the rest of this chapter I'll list and discuss these structure types, and tell you how to fish them.

Subsurface Obstructions to Flowing Water

A ledge in a coastal river; an underwater sandbar that looks like an ocean tide rip; a drop-off at the place where a stream enters a shoreline—these all give an important advantage to bass. Because water cannot be compressed, it moves out of the way of obstructions in its path. As water passes through an area of obstructions it must

slow down and twist and turn to move around and fill in behind everything in its path. The movement as it passes over lumps in the bottom is often marked by standing waves usually referred to as **rip lines.** What happens is that the current flow accelerates under water up the incline formed by the structure. When the rapidly moving water

Figure 67   Dave Rimmer holds the then 20-pound-class world record 33-pound striper. Note the line of tide rip behind him; he is miles from the nearest shore. (Photo by Dave Rimmer)

reaches the top of the incline, it bulges at the surface, causing the visible waves, boils, and whirlpools. Here the striper, especially the big striper, is at home.

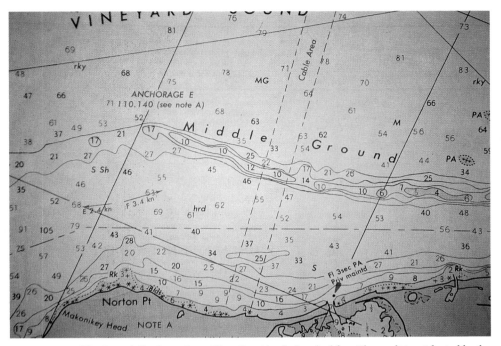

Figure 68   *Middle Ground Shoal goes from 50' to 5' inside of a hundred feet. The result is a tide rip like the one appearing behind Dave Rimmer in figure 65. Note the 3.4 knots of current on the incoming (flood) tide compared to only 2.4 knots on the ebb. The stronger tide is likely to fish better.* (Photo by the author)

In such a situation, fish may lie in several places. First, as the current heads up the incline or into the face of a boulder, the water near the bottom becomes slowed and confused in its direction, because it tumbles around every imperfection along the way. So bass may lie here in front of the main obstruction. Their main lie, though, is typically just in back of the upper lip of the obstruction. If the obstruction lies somewhat perpendicular to the current flow, the fish are likely to be poised in different locations along the ridge that they select based on many potential variables, including depth, temperature of water, proximity to the fastest current, and things you can't see, like the exact configuration of the bottom in any one place. At the top of the structure water flows backward and down, filling in the gap left by the water shooting upward off the end of the plain (which caused the rip in the first place). Here, in just the perfect spot, a bass can hold effortlessly in position while surveying the narrow gap of water rushing by overhead, waiting for weak-swimming baitfish to tumble by.

How do you pick the right structure and the right location along it (Fig. 69)? The key is to look for structure that provide great changes in depth, are in the depth comfort zone for bass, and are in or very near the strongest current flow. There are places like the famous north rip off Block Island, which holds a lot of bass—but at a

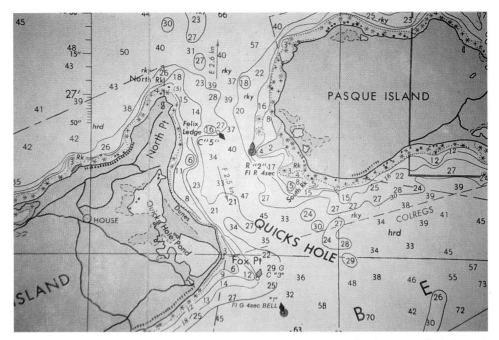

Figure 69   Quick's Hole has excellent structure in several places. The 16-foot hump at Felix ledge and the shallow finger running out to the red buoy are both adjacent to much deeper water and positioned directly in both of the currents flowing down the channel. World records have come from Quick's Hole. (Photo by the author)

depth of 50 or more feet. I believe that any depth over 20 feet becomes really tough on a fly rodder. The right combination might be a large shoal that marks the edge of a turn in a major channel where the depth goes from 40 to 15 feet very abruptly, and the water is moving at 3 knots. The wrong place might be a ledge that comes right to the surface, tucked in back of a point of land, well out of the current's major flow. You need a place where food is likely to constantly be moving past a structure that will make it vulnerable—and at a depth that's fishable with a fly rod.

One of the single most important devices you can own for this type of fishing is a depth recorder. I turn mine on when I get in the boat and off when I get back to the dock. With practice you will see where the fish are as you drift over them. The presence or absence of visible fish on the machine will help you decide whether to move or to switch flies and try again. Your depth recorder allows you to learn about the bottom the way your eyes show you the surface features. Most of the new machines have an automatic setting that keeps the bottom on the screen, and will clearly reveal even a small bass in 40 feet of water.

For most of this fishing a fast-sinking-head line like the L.L. Bean Superhead is the right choice. The fish will not often move from a lie 15 feet under water to take a

Figure 70   This ledge continues out underwater and the water rushing by it creates the obvious surface disturbances. It holds bass—and at fly-roddable depth! (Photo by Harvey Wheeler)

surface offering. Even if stripers are feeding on the surface, they will usually take a subsurface offering—in fact, the bigger fish usually prefer it. This is not to say that they won't feed on the top in a rip; sometimes the sky above a rip is filled with birds, indicating surface feeding. Go ahead and cast a floating line in the rip if you want surface action. A lot depends on your goal. More productivity and bigger fish will usually come to the sinking-line technician, but I know many anglers who would rather take one on top than a dozen underneath. Your choice.

I personally do a lot of deep structure fishing in Maine's Kennebec River. To make the proper presentation you must take several factors into account (Fig. 71). Let's say you have located on a chart a shell bar on the edge of a channel on a turn in the river, with current that flows directly onto it. You can see that the there is an underwater pass 20 feet deep at midtide, located between two humps that are a short distance apart. You want to fish this lie on the dropping tide, because the current doesn't flow onto it on the incoming. (It is important to realize that a structure may fish well on one tide but not the other; it depends on how the structure lies in the path of the current.) You need to get far enough upcurrent that your fly will have sunk to the correct depth before it arrives in the bass's strike zone, and you must allow for any wind that is present. In deciding how long to let your fly sink, there is no substitute for trial and error, tempered with the judgment that comes

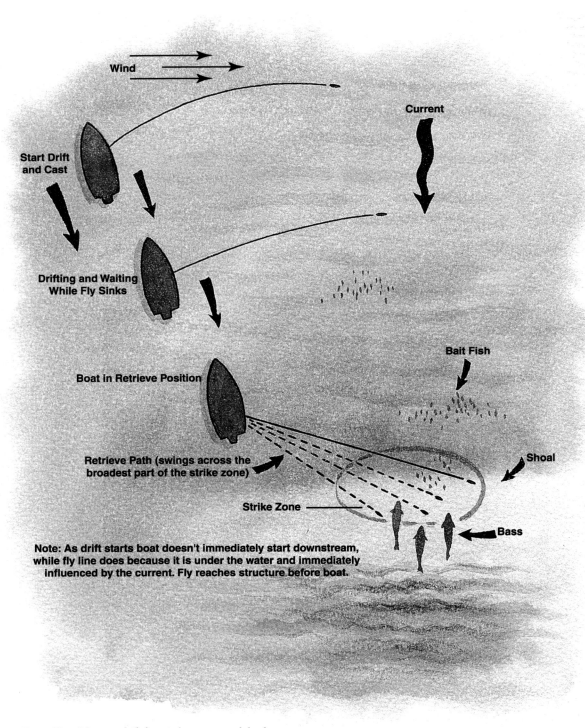

Wind

Current

**Start Drift
and Cast**

**Drifting and Waiting
While Fly Sinks**

Bait Fish

Boat in Retrieve Position

**Retrieve Path (swings across the
broadest part of the strike zone)**

Shoal

Strike Zone

Bass

**Note: As drift starts boat doesn't immediately start downstream,
while fly line does because it is under the water and immediately
influenced by the current. Fly reaches structure before boat.**

Figure 71   Adjusting drift for wind, current, and depth.

from experience. On page 47 I discussed the sinking speeds of various lines. There are a number of other factors, several of which I'll discuss below, that can also influence the sink rate. I put all of these variables into the equation, make my best guess, and count slowly to determine a consistent sinking time for each cast. If in repeated passes at a certain depth you don't touch bottom, then try counting a little longer, or vice versa.

If you are casting to structure from a boat in wind or current, you must be aware of the effects that these forces will have on your presentation. First, if you are anchored, a cast made uptide will have time to sink before you start to retrieve. If you cast downtide, though, your fly line will almost immediately straighten out and come tight. The current will then plane your line up toward the surface, and your fly will not reach feeding depth. In fact, even if you cast into still water, your fly line will sink more quickly if you feed out slack line instead of holding on to it.

If you are drifting without wind, you will move over the bottom at the same speed as the surface water. This creates essentially the same conditions as fishing in still water. The water near the bottom is, however, moving more slowly than the water on the surface. Therefore, if you cast downtide, your fly will be overtaken by your line as they sink to the bottom. This will in effect shorten your cast and force you to strip feverishly in order to give any action to your fly. In moving water and without wind, you are better off casting across the current.

Wind changes everything in striper fishing. What you should do depends on the direction of the wind relative to the direction of the current. The basic rule is to cast at least a few degrees into the wind. This allows time for your fly to sink before your boat's motion tightens the line. To cover every possible combination of current and wind direction would be unwarranted. You must, however, cast in such a way that your fly has time to sink before the line tightens, and so that your boat doesn't drift on top of the line.

The bulk of your fly can also impede the sinking rate of your line. At the end of your sinking time the fly will be farther up in the water column than the belly of your line. This isn't as bad as it seems, however, since the head of the line will have ceased to sink if it is lying on the bottom, and the elevation of your fly may keep it from hanging up once you start to strip. The changing depth of the fly during your retrieve adds to its realism, too. The exception to all this is the first cast of a drift, if you make it while the boat is still coasting to a stop. In the Kennebec I fish from a 25-foot center console. It takes quite a while after I put the boat in neutral before the current stops the forward motion of this heavy craft and compels it to drift at the same speed as the surface water. For my first cast, then, conditions are the same as if the boat was in a wind strong enough to blow it back against the current. If you want any depth and distance in your retrieve under this scenario, you must either cast well up- and across current, or make a very short cast downstream and simply feed out line without tension until the boat's forward motion stops. A lot of technique and knowledge must be put to use by the successful sinking-line fisherman.

My first drift is frequently off the mark, and I simply try again until I get where I want to be. Watch your depth recorder during these drifts, since charts cannot reproduce all the detail that actually exists in a small area. You will find lots of good spots by fishing out your drifts, and by looking at the bottom through your adopted eyes. Also, take note of surface features to show you where a drift started (lobster trap buoys are great for this) and where you hooked up or marked fish on the machine. If no buoys are nearby, triangulate a position from shore points like trees or buildings. GPS coordinates will bring you to a general area but are not accurate enough to help you make repeat drifts over detailed structure.

The types of structure I'm discussing are often vigorous environments. If small baits are present, it is unlikely that bass feeding on current-swept structure will be attracted to them. It is also more likely that you'll find herring, mullet, menhaden, or squid in the ocean rips, and herring or menhaden in the larger estuaries. Once detected, a robust bait like this will try hard to get away, so use long, quick strips to emulate a panicked baitfish. Also, remember that a baitfish of this size swimming at flank speed is sure to displace some serious water. I like a fly similar to the Groceries, which has the size, shape, and heavy-duty action to fill the bill. One of the great things about fishing this turbulent water, especially in the over-10-foot depth range, is that it can be more productive than other types during the height of day. If big stripers are your goal, putting in your time around deeper structure will be one of your best bets.

When you're examining a body of water (especially an urban one) for likely striped bass holding water, it's helpful to be imaginative. Not all structure is the typical ledge or sandbar. I live near the head-of-tide on a Maine river. Every spring flood brings trees and limbs from upriver and deposits many of them where the currents slow as they enter the tidal estuary. In the early summer there are lots of school stripers in the river, and on the dropping tide they take up stations behind submerged and partially submerged debris. In the mouth of the Hudson River the driftwood is joined by shopping carts, cars, construction debris, old wharf pilings, and the inevitable junk gleaned from flowing through one of the world's most populous

Figure 72   Inlet and jetties.

reaches. If you could observe the bottom of the Hudson on some falling tide you'd no doubt witness an army of hungry bass resting in the eddies created by the current's passage through all of this debris. The feeding stripers would rush the baitfish from these man-made feeding stations just as happily as if they were pristine glacial boulders. In some places you'll need a depth finder to see the jagged bottom; in others structure may reach to the surface, or at least cause a visible commotion in the surface of the passing water. If the nearby waters hold stripers, virtually all obstructions to their flow, whether man-made or natural, will be inhabited by the bass.

Inlets and Outlets

When I think of outlets, I always remember a night Phil Perrino and I spent in early November 1992 on the south beach of Martha's Vineyard. On that island, the brackish-water ponds that line this south side are still wild. They fill to several feet

Figure 73   This Maine tidal river exits though a low tide beach. A 68-pound striper was caught here in 1981. (Photo by Dave Rimmer)

above sea level with the fall rains, and then break through to the beach during winter storms. But sometimes the town shellfish commission's backhoe stands in for Mother Nature: Municipalities often open the ponds in the late autumn to allow the herring

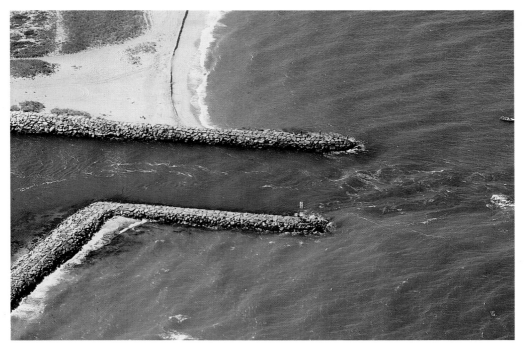

Figure 74   A large inlet complete with jetties; note the strong rip between the jetties. (Photo by Pip Winslow)

Figure 75   As obvious a seam as I've ever seen. (Photo by Dave Rimmer)

and crabs spawned in the ponds to reach the ocean. These openings can be rumored for days in advance, and therefore may be quite crowded with anglers, despite the long drives down the beach to reach them.

This November night, cold and with a howling northwest wind, we were alone. With each small wave that hit the beach, young herring leaving the pond through the narrow opening were splashed back onto the beach, where they flopped down its face, glinting in the moonlight. Finally, upon reaching the wash, they swam away—many right into the maw of a waiting striper. The bass were there all night, like a waiting line at a great restaurant. They were so close to the beach that in our giddiness we dropped herring into the slough at our feet and watched as the faces of 20-pound bass, turning onto their sides to feed in the shallows, appeared and devoured our offerings.

Whether it's a situation like this one, a creek entering a marsh, or a culvert dumping out through an urban seawall, all inlets function in much the same fashion. The key elements are the bait being swept through a narrow run then borne by the current into the receiving body of water, and the feeding stations that are created by the current's interaction with the structure in the inlet. Look for **seams** (lines caused by the meeting of waters moving in opposite directions) created by the fast water's entry into the receiving body of water, and turbulence caused by boulders, ledges, or sandbars jutting into the water's path, or even the

Figure 76   This inlet/outlet to a Cape Cod salt pond has all kinds of structure. In addition to the current and the jetty, a shoal and tide rip have developed clearly— the dark line just to the right of the end of the jetty. (Photo by the author)

funnellike entry to the inlet's narrows. What all of these situations have in common is a place where the bass can wait with comparative ease, then leap out into the current flow to catch baitfish corralled into a finite area.

Since most inlets along the striper coast are tidal, they flow in the opposite direction when the tide changes. Many inlets fish well on both tides, on both sides of the structure, while others do not.

Figure 77 These anglers are working the tide rips off the points of the shore that is actually part of a large inlet. (Photo by Pip Winslow)

Fishing strategies for inlets can be quite varied, since there is such variation in the scope of these features. In general, however, inlets are not really deep structure. Typically you don't need heavy, deep-sinking heads for inlet fishing—I like inlets a lot for that reason, as well as because they are such good producers. In fact, I would venture to say that nearly all of the inlets from Maine to Hatteras produce stripers during their season. You can, however, make no generalizations about the bait that may be present. A large inlet like Waquoit Bay, on Cape Cod, drains and fills a pair of big coastal ponds, and its warm waters hold everything from menhaden to squid, herring, spearing, and virtually anything else that lives even seasonally in southeastern Massachusetts. You can comfortably fish such an inlet from a large boat, and can effectively use sinking heads and large flies. An inlet like this actually has other structure—like bars, points, and flats—confined within it. By contrast, not far down the road Little Pond has a narrow, shallow opening and offers mostly small baitfish, though not always small stripers. For simplicity's sake, then, I'll confine my discussion here to inlets whose main attraction is the narrow stream of current leaving one and entering another body of water; all the other structure that may be present will receive separate treatment in this chapter. In fact, most large feeding areas can be broken down into several different kinds of feeding stations; approaching an area by fishing the individual structure that it contains is often your most productive plan.

While inlets of all sizes can be fished from a boat, the stealth of shore fishing provides the most pleasant, effective way to handle many of them. Pay special attention to the areas where the outflow enters the receiving body of water. Look for changing color, where variances in depth exist. Often a bar will form where the deeper channel of the inlet drops its sand load. Seams formed by the fast water entering the slow also make great places to toss your fly. Be careful to anticipate a strike as your retrieve nears the shore, since the shoreline itself is one of the most likely feeding stations for bass. It is also wise to avoid clambering immediately to the outermost rock, or making the deepest possible wade, then beating the surface with water hauls in pursuit of 90-foot casts. Walk up quietly and fish the waters at your feet carefully—the bass may be right there. Conversely, there are times when shallow water extends out farther than you can wade, and the bass feed at drop-offs outside your casting zone. A technique that has worked for me is to cast out and across the current, then feeding line and even my backing into the flow until my fly is in the strike zone. Don't be quick to strip your fly in from the current. I've often taken a good fish by allowing my fly to fish on its own, undulating in the current's flow, without imparting any further action myself. Frequently, fish hold in the outlet funnel, above the inlet's narrows. (For you trout fishermen, this is the tail of the pool.) Fish also hold along the slower-moving shoreline edge water, or in the eddies around rocks or bars under the water. Cast across the current and let your fly swing across the opening. Effective presentations in all of the above scenarios can require lines of various weights and sinking rates, depending on the depth of the water. Often, however, a floating line is fine, and it has one big advantage: Floating or near-surface presentations frequently reveal to you the presence of stripers. Many times a surface presentation of mine has yielded a roll or flash, which I could then go to work on with other flies, presentation angles, and styles of retrieve, eventually catching the fish. On the other hand, you'll never see a refusal 10 feet under the surface. If two casters are prospecting the same water together, one should use a floating line until you learn that it isn't effective.

The baitfish often found around these smaller or shallow inlets are small or slim. Spearing are perhaps the most common and sand eels probably second, while immature fish of all kinds are often present inside the draining estuary, as are the ever-present grass shrimp. As a general rule, I start with a moderate-size search pattern like a white Deceiver of perhaps 3 or 4 inches, but my first change is likely to be a decrease in size. My experience is that picky fish are seldom seduced by larger, more aggressive patterns. One notable exception to this is when stripers are going

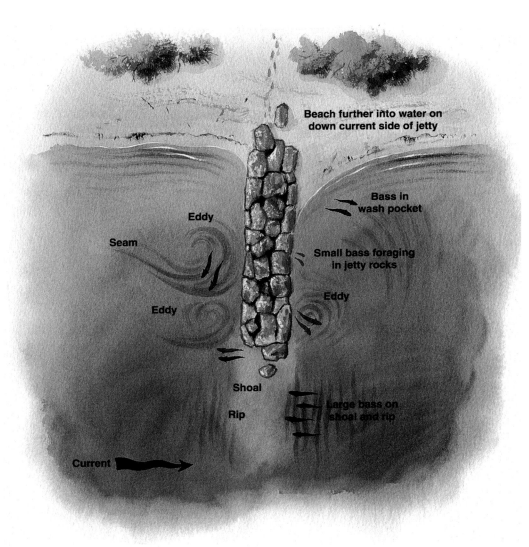

Figure 78   Jetty from beach.

berserk on a large, dense school of bait. Under these circumstances, a large fly allowed to sink under the ruckus then rapidly stripped will often draw a strike. I call this the contrarian approach; it's worth a try, but I wouldn't depend on it. More frequently, thankfully, you need to "match the hatch," and I say "thankfully" because it's the discerning nature of the bass that makes it such a compelling quarry. You may not have to offer an exact replica of the baitfish, but a good facsimile of its silhouette and behavior will often draw a strike. Pay attention to breaking fish. Are the strikes wild surface smashes that signify frantically fleeing fish? Or are they subsurface boils that may be the lazy takes of stripers eating spawning worms? On one trip, casting in a

Figure 79   One of these jetties, originally installed to halt erosion, is now well underwater. Its end is the large black rock out in the middle of the water. This is a great fishing area.

salt pond, I went hitless until I spied a striper **mooning**, or flashing over on her side as she used the flat side of her face to feed right on the bottom. A small Clouser fished slowly near the bottom produced steady action.

A **jetty** is a man-made structure, typically of rock, designed to halt erosion (Fig. 78). At a time when beach erosion was less well understood than today, many jetties were built along the beaches of developing areas to slow shore currents. While it turns out that jetties don't stop erosion, they do change the shapes of the beaches upon which they're built. Prevailing currents dig sand from one side of the jetty and deposit it onto the other. In many ways such structure functions like points on a beach (see page 124). Many inlets are flanked by two jetties to keep them from silting in.

Jetties often make wonderful fishing platforms and fish-holding structure. Look for current seams and back eddies spinning off the sides of jetties, and **pockets** (small, deep-water areas of recessed shoreline) formed between the jetties and the shore. These areas of confused water hold bass the way any submerged structure does. The rock piles themselves can hold stripers, since small fish and crabs often call them home. The best part of most inlet jetties is the end, around which the current bends. Bass will wait right at the tip for bait coming out of both the inlet and the downtide in the main body of water. Large jetties give you the option of casting sinking heads and large flies, the best medicine for big fish.

Inlets give you a place to start. If you are fishing an unknown area that has salt ponds, creeks, rivers, or narrows entering another body of water, start your search there. If fish are in the area, such places are almost sure to hold them.

Bridges

Bridges are an important and unique type of structure. What they offer stripers boils down to pilings, abutments, and shadows. **Pilings** and **abutments** are simply obstructions, similar to boulders. Water piling into them causes a dead spot of noncompressible water on the upcurrent side, a back eddy on the downcurrent side, and seams on both sides. Bass can use these places to hold, and they do. The trick is to make your presentation in a way that keeps your line from wrapping around the structure. You must be careful and accurate with your casts. A bait-fishing friend of mine once told me of a bridge abutment that held huge bass. "At the midpoint of the ebb tide," said my friend, "you must drop your eel within 6 inches of the cement, let it drop straight to the bottom, and you'll get a fish if one is there." My take on the situation was that dropping

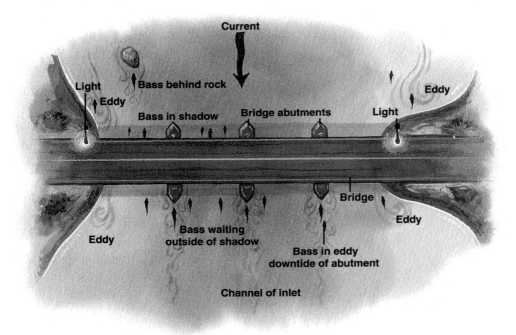

Figure 80   Bridge structure.

Figure 81   Water piles into this stone corner as it rushes under a small bridge. Bass hold in this fan-shaped area of disturbed water and wait for a meal. (Photo by the author)

the eel any farther than 6 inches would cause it to be swept away from the piling before it got into the strike zone. I know you can't do this with a fly, and you don't always have to, but the closer you can come the better. This is a place for a Clouser with very heavy eyes, tied sparsely so that it will sink quickly.

Shadows are, however, quite different. In the early summer of 1965, I spent more than a few nights fishing under the light that illuminated the sign of a furniture company beside a Damariscotta River bridge. Each night herring would gather under that light. Like a textbook illustration, a 4-foot bass would hold 10 feet downcurrent from them in the clearly defined shadow of the bridge. Every now and then a herring dropped a little too far back and entered the shadow; without hesitation, the bass would bolt forward to inhale it. Within 30 seconds the bass would again rise into view, finning patiently in the shadow of the bridge. Conversely, around a bridge near my Cape Cod stomping grounds, bass wait in changing light on both the uptide and downtide sides. On one side they wait for baitfish to enter the shadow; on the other they wait for them to leave it. These bass are clearly taking advantage of the

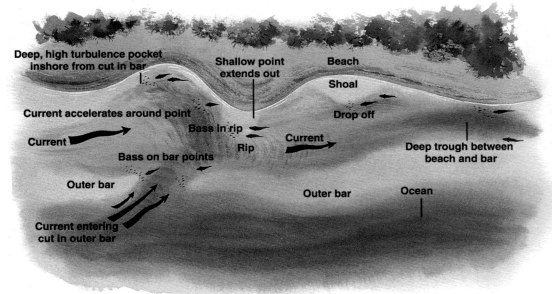

Figure 82   Beach with outer bar structure.

baitfish's initial confusion upon entering the changed light zone to feed on them. (The bass may also be confused by the changing light, but less so than the baitfish just entering the zone.)

While I've only worked a few bridges, my observation on all of them is that a good-size fly—one larger than the baitfish present—will work just fine. In fact, I have been refused under a bridge on small offerings that duplicated the spearing bass were feeding upon, even though 100 yards away in a little eddy the flies worked perfectly. One thing that is unique about a shadow structure is its inverse relationship to water depth. This structure is present on the surface, but probably not on the bottom. At night along the Chesapeake Bay Bridge Tunnel, stripers of all sizes can be caught on a floating line. On some nights an unusual kind of sight fishing is available in which you cast to individual fish visible in the shadows. The shoreside abutments of a bridge often create a narrowing of the waterway. The currents flowing past such structure are similar to those of any point and may be important feeding stations.

Beaches and Shorelines

If striped bass are the royalty of East Coast inshore fishing, then a sand beach is the plushest room in the castle. The greatest spot on earth is a back beach on a warm June evening with sand eels wriggling about your feet. As you wade and cast, you can detect stripers by their lazy feeding movements, faintly visible in the moonlight.

Figure 83   This angler has hooked a good bass from Maine's rocky shoreline. Note the moving water off the tip of this rock. (Photo by Harvey Wheeler)

Their great tails and broad shoulders create boils and rippling rings in the water. This is the soul of fly fishing for striped bass—not to knock the rest of it, as in fact I do very little of this style of fishing, which isn't available around every corner. I love it all—as perhaps you do or will—but sand-beach fishing is the pinnacle of the sport.

At first glance the fishiness of many beaches is hidden by their simplicity, but looks can be deceiving. Nor are all beaches simple to behold. The boulder-strewn shores of the Elizabeth Islands, for example, where currents flow at more than 3 knots, are beaches. New Jersey's Island Beach Park with its steep, heavy surf is a beach, as is little Eastville Beach, completely contained within Vineyard Haven Harbor on Martha's Vineyard. For purposes of this chapter even Maine's rockbound coast is a beach. The reason for lumping together all of these seemingly disparate locations is that their fish-holding features all share common threads, which I'll explore. As I pointed out earlier, all feeding stations give predators an advantage over their prey. You simply need to identify, in any structure, the various feeding areas that are present.

Every shoreline is constantly under siege from the water that it borders. The level of this activity varies greatly, but in all cases the shoreline is sculpted by the water. This sculpting yields several distinct types of features: bars (both inner and outer), cuts between bars, points, deep pockets, and troughs or sloughs. These are all elements of both sand and gravel beaches. Rocky, or even ledge, shorelines have some of these same features; also, along many beaches rocks are detached from the shore-line, providing additional feeding locations. Each kind of structure can, in its own way, be attractive to baitfish, and also provide feeding advantages to predators like the striper.

Perhaps the most obvious feature you can find on a beach is a **point.** Points are caused by the actions of currents and waves along a shore. Usually they're built of sand or gravel gathered at the expense of the adjacent shoreline, leaving a hole or pocket. The material is scoured out by the water and deposited on the point, which is located downtide in the direction of the prevailing current. Currents must accelerate around the point, which usually extends outward under water. This creates feeding stations in the form of current-swept drop-offs. A similar situation is created by waves moving in and out over changing depths.

To a degree, the periods of faster current that come from full- and new-moon phases and the greater wave action that comes from heightened wind conditions will increase the attraction that these lies have for a predator like the striper. Like all good things, however, it can be overdone. Ten knots of southerly wind blowing onto a south-facing beach can be much better than a dead calm; 30 knots will quickly build

Figure 84   Look at the steep angle of this beach; there is excellent water right at your feet. (Photo by Dave Rimmer)

unfishable, dirty water (full of suspended sediment). To a large degree you can treat a point of land similarly to an ocean tide rip; in fact, rips often extend from beachfront points (Great Point on Nantucket is a prime example). Stripers, however, don't need to rest in an eddy along the average beach point, because the flowage just isn't that strong. For stripers, the fact that any prey moving along the beach is forced into the turbulent shallows of a point is reason enough to be there; still, they could be found anywhere around the point, not just tucked in tight to a particular feeding station.

Very few beaches are so steep that they warrant a fast-sinking head. An intermediate line is my favorite: It casts better in the wind and it sinks a little. This last quality helps it resist the movements made by a floating line fished in strong winds and breaking surf. Don't wade right in; make your initial casts close to the beach. Cast your fly so that wind, current, and wave action will combine to make your fly swing naturally through the probable strike zone. It may take a cast or two to achieve the proper presentation, but the fish could be anywhere, and no cast is wasted. When it comes to fishing beaches, points are your second most dependable bet—after inlets.

Next on the list are **bars.** Like points, bars are created by suspended material dropped by moving water. Not all beaches have discernible bars. On the other hand, some, like the great outer Cape Cod beaches, have very obvious outer bars complete

Figure 85   Between this beach and the well-formed outer bar is a deep and turbulent trough—possibly full of stripers, especially at night. (Photo by Dave Rimmer)

with channels or cuts between sections of them. Typically, outer bars are found on direct oceanfront beaches where heavy waves dig sand from the shore. As the water escapes back to sea, sand is deposited where the water slows down. Since the waves come ashore over the bars with considerable velocity, especially during an onshore blow, the water needs additional drainage from the area between the bar and the shore. As a result, water returning to the sea excavates canals, called **cuts,** through the bars. Often these bars and cuts are clearly visible, but in some cases they can be hard to see. Depending on the depth of the surrounding water and the exposure to waves and currents, bars may be near or very far from shore. In some cases bars may reach right onto the beach, with only a small, deep cut between them from the beach. Bars and cuts are also constantly changing in size and location. Many beaches look entirely different in the spring than they do in the fall, because they've been sculpted by winter storms. The best way to find bars and cuts is to spend time looking at the beach during low tide on a sunny day. The bars are the light-colored areas; the deeper cuts or channels are comparatively dark. It is not unusual, especially on extra-low tides, for some outer bars and even their troughs to bare completely.

The currents flowing along the beach, and the waves pouring back and forth over the bars and through the cuts, create a variety of feeding situations. Many of these are big-water structure where it's tough for the fly fisher to be as efficient as the plug caster. This is not always the case, though, especially if you don't waste time in water that doesn't lend itself to fly fishing. Look instead for places where bars extend close to shore; here you can cast into the current-filled cuts between bar and shore. And in some cases, you can wade (with great caution) at low tide to outer bars, and fish the cuts on their ends or the oceanfront beyond. Such outside structure can be broken down into the same inlets, points, and underwater features that I've already discussed.

Pockets are another type of beach structure. Like points, they occur on both rocky and sandy beaches. Pockets often occur where the shore has clear exposure to incoming waves, and no bar or offshore ledge offers nearby protection. The waves retain their height until they're very near the beach. When waves like this hit the beach, the steep angle causes erosion and removes sand, which is carried by currents downtide to the next point or bar. One night years ago on Block Island, I discovered that the fish were not at the tip of Southwest Point—their frequent location. Instead, they were 20 feet from shore in a steep-sided pocket immediately adjacent to the point. Had I been casting flies that night instead of using a spinning rod, I could have hooked a number of bass of between 30 and 40 pounds.

At night, baitfish often hug the beach, where they are safe from many of their predators. Couple the presence of this bait, especially in a deep hole, and the turbulence caused by the high volume of water coming and going through the pocket, and you have striper heaven. And the best action in these pockets is frequently in the **wash,** or frothy turbulence caused by the waves' direct contact with the beach. Breaking waves mix large volumes of air with the water, and create what surf fishers call white water. Fish your fly carefully through this white water, since many strikes will come right there. Pockets are easy to spot, even at night, since the white tops of their breaking waves are closer to shore than those forming on shallower water; also, the beach in the pocket is likely to be obviously steeper.

If the wash is one of the prime feeding zones along the beachfront, then the **trough** is the staging area. Immediately in back of the wash and before the outer bar is a deeper slough or trough. Here, safe in the deeper water, predators lurk between forays into the wash. In some cases you will not be able to cast completely across a wash. In others, however, you will be able to reach all the way across the trough to the outer bar. The stage of the tide, the wind, and the beach's orientation toward the open sea all affect the distances involved. In the trough your fly will be pushed at you with the incoming wave, then sucked away from you in the aftermath of a breaker as water rushes off the beach, back into the trough. I strip a bit faster when the wave pushes toward me to keep a tight line and to impart action, but I sometimes stop my retrieve or even let line slip backward through my fingers to mimic a hapless baitfish overpowered by the undertow. In conditions of wave action like this, it is typically more effective to use a good-size fly with a lot of action and the ability to move some water. To effectively fish pockets 8 or 10 feet deep, I like to use an intermediate or even a sinking-tip rather than a floating line. Stripers foraging in the turbulence of breaking waves are more likely to expend the energy required to catch a baitfish if the reward is a sufficient amount of calories. While I'm sounding a bit like a broken record, I suggest starting your search with a 4- or 5-inch white Deceiver.

In many areas along the coast you will find boulders or ledges along the beaches. The waves or currents that wash by such structure should be fished in essentially the same way as offshore bars or deep-water structure. Along the Elizabeth Islands, the shore is crammed with boulders, some visible, some deep and out of sight. As I drift by these rocks I cast and retrieve to individual large boulders as if they were boulders in a trout stream. Fish find protection among these rocks, forage for crabs, and hold in the eddies that they create, waiting for baitfish to move by. If the water is sufficiently deep and I know there are boulders all along the bottom, I prospect with large flies like Groceries or even bunker flies, cast on heavy sinking lines. If, on the other hand, the water is less than 10 feet deep, a floating line may reveal the presence of fish that refuse your fly. In general, however, I believe that more and larger bass can be taken if you retrieve close to the actual depth of the striper's lie.

Most of what I have just said relates to boat fishing. In very few locations will you find water deeper than 10 feet within a fly cast of the shoreline, and even if you do you will probably find very shallow water somewhere during your retrieve. Most shorelines are not places for a 400-grain head. Under conditions of low light, fish will often move in from the boulders offshore to feed on baitfish like sand eels or spearing living along the shoreline. Since fish feeding on this thin bait can be picky, you may find yourself working with tiny flies and floating lines just inside the areas where boat fishermen cast heavy, deep-water flies.

Some areas—Cape Ann, Massachusetts, for instance, and most of the Maine coast—were treated roughly by retreating glaciers, leaving coastlines of solid, jagged **ledge.** Despite the apparent disparity between sand and rock, the differences to you as a fly caster will be quite small. If you started with a sand beach and by a snap of the fingers could lock it permanently in position, you would have the equivalent of a rocky shoreline. One big difference, however, is that farther east in Maine, beyond Cape Small, much of the water is often very deep near the shore. Add this to the fact that this far east the striper migration starts thinning out and your surf-casting chances are greatly diminished, though not eliminated. Ledge shorelines have points, cuts between ledges, scoured-out holes or pockets, and offshore rocks to provide additional structure. They do not have outer bars, but the offshore ledges can work the same way. Attack these rocky shores just the way you would any beach, by breaking them down into the pieces that I've discussed. The exception is that the depth along many of these rocky shorelines allows you to fish even from the shore with heavy sinking lines, and to prospect near the bottom for larger fish. A word of caution is warranted: Deep water means larger waves breaking close to the beach. Being knocked off your feet on the sand is one thing; slipping on rocks and then being pounded into them by waves is quite another. Be careful; watch the water for a while before you step out onto the rocks. There are many excellent fishing spots along the Maine coast that I simply won't fish at night.

Sod Banks and Marshy Shorelines

A great deal of striper fishing is done in estuaries that have marshy shorelines. The warm shallows of marshes and the decaying plant matter contained within them

Figure 86   Drainage creeks such as this one provide excellent fishing, particularly on the ebb tide when the marsh baitfish are funneled toward the channel. (Photo by Dave Rimmer)

are the foundation of the coastal food chain. In general—though not always— marshes are the province of smaller fish. In season, however, large bass enter creeks to feed on the herring and menhaden that themselves are feeding on the tiny creatures that exist in the marshes in such abundance. Sometimes large bass will follow the anadramous herring to their spawning runs. If they are present, big bass may give themselves away by boiling on the surface of a creek as they chase large baits. Usually, though, small stripers are quietly working along the steep and/or undercut marsh banks, feeding on grass shrimp, worms, juvenile fish, or small baits like spearing.

If you cannot see feeding fish your best course of action is to fish the structure. The best place to work any structure is in moving water. Examine a marsh sod bank and you'll find some structure, like points, that you already know how to deal with (see page 124). Often you'll find inlets that drain the back marshes that you also know how to work (see page 114). Sometimes, however, broad sections of marsh deposit bait into the estuary as the tide drops. While marshy shorelines may fish well on water moving in either direction, most estuaries produce better on ebb tides. There is more velocity to the water, since the salt water must be drained out, along with any fresh water that has entered the estuary. These combine to increase the volume of water that must pass through the estuary's outlet in a finite time. Again, stripers feeding on grass shrimp dropping out of the spartina grasses may occasionally be visible as they feed. Prospecting miles of seemingly quiet shoreline is very time consuming, of course; look for the places that baitfish, and therefore stripers, collect.

One structure that is unique to the marshy shore is the **undercut bank.** (This needs no introduction to trout anglers.) Here, out of sight of predators, the striper waits for baitfish to be swept into a tube that has only one open side. The bank doesn't even have to be undercut; it can just be deep and subjected to a direct exposure to the

Figure 87   The steep side of this marsh bank allowed this angler to locate stripers that had pushed baitfish against its edge. (Photo by Dave Rimmer)

available current. A sinking fly, like a Clouser, can quickly drop right into the strike zone. Make your cast close to the shore and let the fly swing into the feeding lane. In fact, bass are sometimes so close to the shore that you easily scare them with your approach; a soggy marsh readily transmits the sound of your footsteps. One expert at this type of fishing makes his first casts 20 feet back from the water's edge; several feet of his fly line are frequently on the marsh grass as he starts his retrieve.

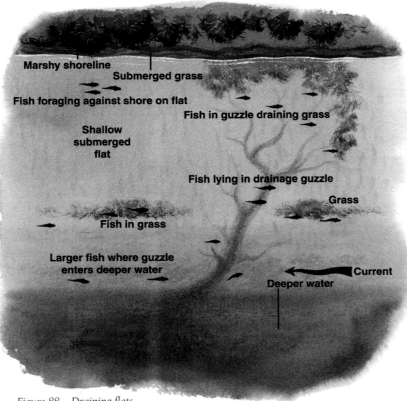

Figure 88   *Draining flats.*

Another hint of the presence of predators and prey is attention from birds. A likely shoreline that is covered with gulls, or a point that has four great blue herons stationed on it, is far more likely to contain fish than a similar area void of apparent life.

Flats and Sight Fishing

Twenty years or so ago, Bob Pond, maker of the Atom plug, told me a story about fishing in Cape Cod Bay. It seems that a charter-boat captain whom Bob knew found a place where on the dropping tide stripers could be seen leaving a large sand flat. These fish, however, refused everything thrown in their path. Bob was confident that his plugs would take these fish, but he soon found out otherwise. Finally, in desperation, he cast directly at the tail end of one of the fish. The 20-pound bass wheeled around and attacked the plug—purely a self-defense tactic, in Bob's view. The big news was, of course, the availability of stripers (and big ones at that) on those expansive sand flats. The hardware fishermen of that era probably had no lure that effectively

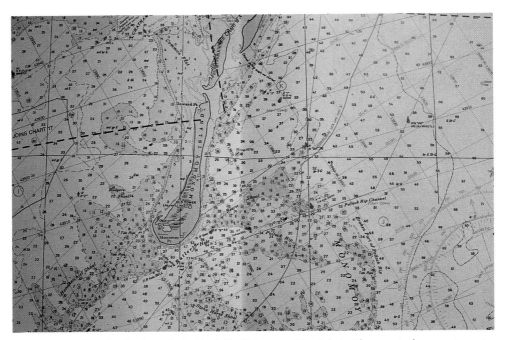

Figure 89   Look at the shoals on the inside (left) of Monomoy Island, but with access to deeper water, cuts, tide rips, and more. (Photo by Pip Winslow)

mimicked the sand eels or small crabs those bass were feeding on. Certainly they were feeding—why would they abandon the safety of the deep water except to eat?

In recent years I've heard more and more about stripers being fished bone-fish style, on the flats. Significant flats fisheries exist off Plum Island, Monomoy Island, Nantucket Island, Dogfish Bar off Martha's Vineyard, and Gardiners Bay in Long Island Sound. I'm certain that the shallow bays of the mid-Atlantic hold many locations suitable for flats fishing for stripers. Still, in my travels and conversations with fishermen in this area, I found little activity in striper flats fishing. Perhaps this is still a fishery yet to be discovered. Flats fishing appeals to the soul of many fly fishers, since the angler is as intimate with the fish as possible. Inside that thin, clear wrapper formed by its watery element the bass can live; outside, even 1 inch, it suffocates. The angler sees the striper moving along in this shallow water window; carefully he casts a fly in front of the fish and lets it sink to the bottom; the fish bolts forward, perhaps turns on its side, and takes the offering. Upon discovery of the angler's treachery, the bass hurtles across the flats at flank speed, straining for the safety of deep water. Even if the fly is refused, the intimacy with this beautiful creature is a satisfying reward in itself. Contrast this to trolling a multihooked lure 30 feet below the surface on 100 yards of wire line connected to a heavy rod resting in a

Figure 90   No, not Key West—Plum Island, Massachusetts. (Photo by Dave Rimmer)

rod holder. No wonder so many people have come to prefer fly casting for stripers, especially on the flats!

While stripers scavenge randomly over the flats, there is typically a reason for their presence in any particular area. On an incoming tide, stripers may move along grass banks or shorelines, hoping to corner baitfish there. On the drop, stripers may wait for baitfish to be pushed off the flats into channels, or against the edges of bars. As with any flats fishing, stealth is important. On some flats, like Monomoy, anglers can wade along looking for fish; more often, however, the tidal ranges of East Coast flats make wading and sight fishing tough. Afloat, you can achieve the greatest stealth by drifting or poling from a boat like the southern flats hull that has a low noise level and an inconspicuous silhouette. You'll need small flies that mimic the crabs, worms, and small baitfish present here. Big fish, however, like big baits, and a cow-bass may very well jump on a fly that suggests a bunker or herring that has strayed into its path. Even a surface fly may well be effective. Water shallow enough for sight fishing can usually be worked with a floating or intermediate fly line. Flats fishing is one of the best applications for clear fly lines. A pair of good-quality polarized sunglasses is vital to successful sight fishing. I have found that amber gives me the best vision into the water. Low-light angles or cloudy days typically obscure underwater vision. I often start my days with blind casting to structure, then switch over to sight fishing around 10 A.M. Sight casting is certain to grow in importance as a style of striper fishing.

Not all shallow-water flats fishing is sight fishing, though. Areas of flat bottom are present inside estuaries, along beaches, and in the salt ponds and bays that exist in back of many beaches. If you are fishing a shallow area toward evening or on a cloudy day and fish are not showing on the surface, then you need to search by reading the water. Typically the shoreline mirrors the bottom in front of it. For instance, a long grassy point that extends into a salt pond undoubtedly continues under water. Movement in the water may reveal current seams or the confluence of drainage channels. Even without visible fish, prospecting doesn't have to be really blind; it can make use of the educated guess. There is an old law of surf fishing: "Always fish with the wind in your face." Whether you are deciding on which shore of a salt pond to fish, or which side of a point on a beach, the wind should be a big consideration. Wind creates movement in the water that can herd baitfish, or provide a turbulent environment that favors a powerful predator like the striper. All things being equal, try to fish areas on their windward sides, if conditions permit.

Shallow areas like flats or bays allow a great deal of sunshine to enter the water; they warm quickly and support a lot of life, especially if they have a dark bottom. Typically the shallower flats, especially during periods of high sunlight, house small fish. But they can yield excellent action and are a pleasure to fish with light tackle and small, easy-to-cast flies.

I usually search shallow-water flats with a small baitfish fly like a Juve or Deceiver, and a floating line. This way, if a fish makes even a pass at my fly, it reveals itself in the shoal water.

CHAPTER 11

How-To Tips

Shore Fishing

I must admit that shore fishing is my first love. The thing about fly fishing that captures my imagination is making contact with wild fish while presenting a handcrafted fly at the end of a line I hold in my own hand. Standing at the ocean's edge, smelling the sea, and being just another link in the whole, natural, oceanic order of things comprises the perfect atmosphere in which to practice the art of fly fishing.

Assume that you come prepared to a shoreline you've never fished before, having received only one tip: Bass are around. You already know which baitfish species might be present, and which types of feeding stations you should look for. You now have the enjoyable task of finding the productive spots of this shoreline. Start with a chart. Though charts will not show you most small rips or pockets along a beach, they will show you estuaries, inlets, and major points of land. They will also give you an idea of what roads are around, or what other access issues you may face.

Once you locate a major structure, survey the area during the day. Climb up on a boulder or bluff and look for the waves breaking near shore that will indicate a pocket, the shape of an outer bar, or an inlet where fish may hold. If you have a four-wheel-drive vehicle and the proper permits, and you're in an area that allows beach driving, take a spin along the beach. Note the direction of the wind—look for bait schools or birds sitting on the water or beach. If you are just there for one tide you may have to cut back on this investigation, but by all means, before you make a cast, use what you've learned so far to read the water.

After you pick a spot, you select an outfit and head for the water, right? Yes— but first clean and stretch your line. While fly lines have improved since the days of braided hair, they're not perfect yet; review the line-maintenance discussion on page 61. And don't forget your stripping basket—see page 87 for more information.

Now you're almost ready to cast. I like to start with a 4-inch white Deceiver, unless I know that this fly will not be a good facsimile of the baitfish likely to be dominant in the area. This fly is simply the best all-around search pattern I know. The Deceiver wiggles like a fish and has a minnowlike profile; also, white is the belly color of most baitfish. The bucktail on the Deceiver breathes and pulses in the water, attracting fish from a distance.

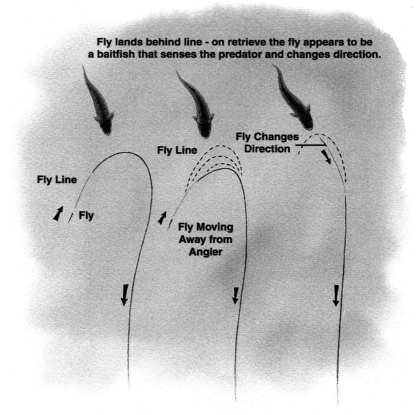

Figure 91   Don't worry if the fly lands behind the fly line on some casts; the fly may appear to be a baitfish that senses the predator and changes direction.

While many of the fish that you will catch are in close, I believe in tossing as long a line as I can without undue strain, until I know that there are no fish beyond the lip of the beach. (Though you don't need tennis elbow, and unless you're a young athlete, I'd suggest wearing one of the arm bands that are sold to combat this condition.) Within the limits of your sustainable capability, why not cast as far as possible? It's likely that any structure a little closer to the refuge of deep water will hold more and larger bass, and you'll cover the close water in your retrieve anyway.

An exception to this strategy is in order, however, for shallow and/or very calm water. Here you may want to alternate your long cast with some very short ones that will not **line** fish (scaring them by slapping your fly line down on the water, or even by letting its shadow pass overhead) close to shore. Another technique that I often employ is to include casts at angles to the beach, including some virtually parallel to the surf line. These casts, combined with some straight out from the shore, will thoroughly cover the water.

I'm also not concerned that my casts land arrow-straight every time. The famed New York bucktail-jig caster Captain John DeMaio said in his book *Fishing with the Bucktail* that one of the most convincing motions a lure can make is to "turn around" (Fig. 91). If on some casts your fly lands in back or to the side of your fly line, it may be a blessing in disguise. It may be the circling of the fly that convinces a monster bass your fly is a confused and terrified baitfish. Besides, every now and then the line will come tight in the air, giving you a few extra feet of retrieve that you wouldn't have had if you hadn't stripped out the extra line to begin with.

And speaking of retrieves, there is a time for the traditional single-handed pull. If you want a long, quick movement, like the one a big bunker would make upon detecting a striper, use the one-handed strip. In boat fishing, except in very high wind, I always retrieve with one hand. From shore, however, and especially into a stripping basket, the shorter pulls of a two-handed retrieve lend themselves to mimicking the smaller baitfish that are often present. I find that I can make a very convincing retrieve by first placing the handle of my rod under my arm, with the tip pointing toward the water; resting my wrists on the edge of and extending over my basket; and stripping in line by pulling it in toward my body then releasing it just as I start the same motion with my other hand (Fig. 92). Because I leave my wrists fixed on the basket, my fingertips move in an arc, and the line "wags" back and forth. Watch the fly as you do this—the wiggle is irresistible, or seems like it should be.

Sometimes the fish are fussy. Suppose that on your second cast you see a bass following behind your fly. Your inclination is probably to slow down, or even stop,

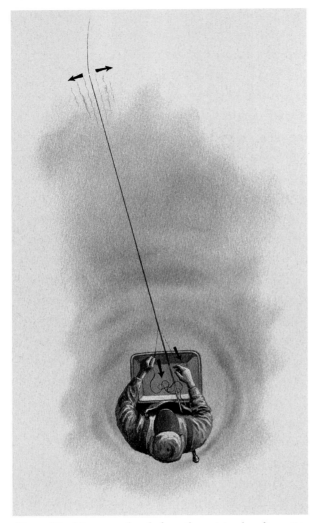

Figure 92   Move your hands from the wrist only; alternating right and left pulls creates a rhythm down the fly line to the fly. This causes the fly to swim back and forth very realistically. Speed and cadence can be varied easily to mimic different-sized baits.

the retrieve—but you should do just the opposite. Don't worry, you cannot take the fly away from this striper. An attacking striper swimming at 15 miles per hour—and they can swim at more than 20—is moving at 22 feet per second. A very fast strip is closer to 4 feet per second. The bass is interested, but for some reason is not ready to eat your fly. Try a long, quick pull, or try just speeding up your retrieve. You want to create the illusion that the meal the bass was taking for granted is now escaping. If you don't get a hit on the next cast or two, try something different. Which way to go depends on a lot of things. If fish are obviously feeding near you, the problem may be that you're simply not imitating the food; try to get a glimpse of the actual bait. Also, I told you earlier that most picky fish require a smaller fly: Usually, they want it presented slower, too. Try dead drifting a small, realistic-looking fly.

What if there is no obvious feeding going on, but you are getting regular follows that don't take? You may be casting to resting fish. This doesn't mean that they won't eat; instead, a change of flies is called for. If the water is less than 15 feet deep, which it will undoubtedly be near shore, try going to the surface. I always have a few poppers (although I'll explain in the final chapter why I dislike them) or Deceivers tied with a spun and clipped deer-hair head. A retrieve right in the surface film doesn't give the bass a clear look at the fly; it may yield a strike when a subsurface retrieve fails. Try different sizes, bigger and smaller, then go down deeper with a Clouser.

Of course, I've also seen times when every fly change I made gave me a fish or two, and then nothing. If this happens to you, try changing the angle of your cast. A baitfish entering the feeding zone from an unnatural angle may make a bass curious but fail to turn on its feeding instincts.

If you run out of tricks and don't want to move, try resting the water for 10 or 15 minutes—it can work wonders. Don't keep pounding the same spot with the same fly without results. I like to move around a lot, and when I do stay put for a while I cover the water in a fan-shaped pattern. Fish are not evenly distributed along a shore-line. A good school may be only yards away from unproductive water. Once you find fish, though, don't be in a hurry to move off. Kenny Vanderlaske's old mentor, a Mon-tauk market fisherman, told him, "Never leave fish to find fish." Sage advice, since even if the fish in front of you are small, the conditions to the liking of the striper are obviously present—stick with it and who knows what will show up.

I'd like to expand on that last thought, too, by noting that the conditions that attract feeding stripers will often repeat themselves in a day (technically, every 24 hours and 50 minutes). It is not unusual to have stripers show up in a certain part of a certain tide rip at the same stage of the tide for several days in a row. Tides along the East Coast occur roughly 50 minutes later each day, however, so all feeding patterns eventually end. The angle of light into the water at the time of the tide phase that ini-tially spawned the feeding spree gradually becomes drastically different. Only during an intense migration of a particular baitfish do I find the same stage of the tide as pro-ductive in 12 hours (high and low tides each occur approximately every 12 hours) as it is in a full day. Author John Cole, one of my frequent fishing companions, is full of anecdotes from his years of commercial fishing for stripers on the east end of Long Island. "They never bite two tides a day" is one such witticism. I have found this to be partially true—a spot in a tide rip will fish much better on one of the two tides than the other. The big bite may simply be taking place at that time somewhere else not far away, because conditions aren't as favorable as they might be in 12 hours. Stripers are also known as "pulse feeders," and will commonly go for periods of time without feeding, followed by regular binges.

As you retrieve, keep your rod tip pointed down toward the water and in the direction of your fly. If you feel a grab, just keep stripping until things become tight before you raise your rod tip. This straight-line technique will force the hook point to penetrate far better than will striking with a comparatively soft rod. If you miss the strike, hesitate for a second; the bass may come back and pick up the baitfish that it assumes it has stunned.

After you hook a striper, you need to decide whether or not to place it on your reel. In my experience, more good fish are lost while trying to get to the reel than are landed because the drag was smoother than the angler's fingers. When I hook a striper it has to earn its way to the reel. Unlike freshwater fishing, you are not likely to pop a leader or rip out a hook by playing the fish on your fingers. Besides, you'll just waste time restripping all that fly line. When first hooked, a bass will often twist and turn in the water, making it difficult for you to keep firm pressure on the line. A useful technique is to simply back up, moving yourself away from the fish. This may help you clear the line to the reel. If you hook the kind of striper that makes it clear it's headed rapidly for your reel, hold the line lightly in your line hand, move that hand out to an arm's length from the reel, and concentrate on the line, trying to anticipate and clear tangles before they get to the guides.

Stripers are excellent and versatile fighters. You can expect very hard pulls, rare jumps, likely surface thrashing, and, in shallow water, some long runs. The striper has, however, nothing sharp with which to cut your line, and its body is not designed for a really long fight. Your greatest risk of losing a big bass exists if rocks are nearby. The striper's tendency is to hug the bottom and wrap you around a rock, cutting you off in the process. If rocks abound, you must put on enough heat to steer the bass away (not always possible) or have luck on your side. Rocks or similar obstacles aside, your biggest assets are patience and having the fish well hooked. The striper has a large mouth lined with soft skin, and tends to engulf the fly with this mouth. During a long fight the hook will frequently shred this soft skin, and the fish will get away. Using a special hook bend (see page 200) is the best way to increase your odds of lip-hooking a bass.

I believe in a fair amount of drag pressure. Perhaps I should suggest getting a scale and setting the drag at 20 or 30 percent of tippet strength, but I simply don't know anyone who actually does this, except for big-game anglers. (Also, after every fish you would have to strip out against several pounds of drag pressure.) I use feel to set my drag at a pressure that's snug but still well under the breaking strength of my tippet. I apply more pressure, if needed, by palming my reel and/or squeezing my line against the rod. Typically, anglers apply far less pressure than they think. When you're doing so, you should never lift the handle of the rod to more than a right angle to the line. Rods are most often broken by lifting the rod tip too high; this transfers the pressure toward the tip, the least-rugged portion of the rod blank. Rather than stress your equipment, then, remember that the longer the fish is out there, the lower your chances of landing it are—and the higher the chances that it will not recover if released.

Figure 93   This low rod angle puts pressure on the fish and keeps it off the more easily broken upper part of the rod.

Once the fish approaches the shore, you face some new challenges. First, if you are up on a rock, you will need to get down closer to the water. I've done a lot of this kind of fishing, and I can tell you that the time to plan your path is in advance. Next season, I pledge that I'm going to carry a telescoping landing net so that I can avoid slippery, weed-covered rocks. If you are on a beach, you must land your fish by using the push of the waves coming ashore to move it out of the water; apply light pressure as the waves recede, and you'll eventually ground it. If you try to hold the fish back against a receding wave, you will often break your line.

Once a striper is within your reach, you need nothing to help you land it but your own hand. Like the largemouth bass, the striper has a lower jaw that makes a perfect handle. Simply insert your thumb in the bass's mouth and pick the fish up, rotating your thumb down and index finger up. The bass will nearly always stop wiggling and hang there with its mouth open to be unhooked. You can lift a really large bass from the water by putting the fingers of both your hands in its mouth and keeping your thumbs outside. A device called the Boga Grip holds the fish securely by the lip while a built-in scale weighs it (Fig. 94). Lifting any fish, especially a big one, from the water, however, is harmful—sometimes deadly—to the fish, and should be avoided if possible. If you need a photo, take it of the fish cradled on the wet sand or

Figure 94   The Boga Grip safely holds stripers while weighing them. (Photo by Duncan Barnes)

with your arm supporting its gut, and avoid putting pressure on its spine or intestines.

Boat Fishing

There are many kinds of boats and, like fly rods, each size and design has benefits for certain kinds of striper fishing. If you are fishing the skinny water back inside a salt pond, then most of what I said about shore fishing is appropriate to boat fishing, since you're still in calm, wadable water. What I'll discuss now, however, are some techniques more applicable to open-water boat fishing, especially for larger bass. While I told you that the shore was my first love, maybe this is partially because I do most of my fishing from a boat, and I relish the variety. Day in, day out, many more big striped bass are landed from boats than from the shore—simply because you have the ability to cover several good spots in one outing, and increased ability to fish structure in proximity to deep water.

Boat fishing, like shore fishing, starts with reviewing charts, not only to find likely spots but also to make sure you stay out of trouble. The rocky shorelines, seething ocean tide rips, and pounding surf lines can be trouble if you are not aware and careful. You also need, however, to study your charts to break down your general fishing areas into the structure that I discussed in chapter 10.

If you're fortunate enough to find big bass pounding away on a school of baitfish, then you'll probably catch them with nearly any fly that you present. Count these experiences, however, as among the most fortunate in your fishing life. Most big bass are going to be picked off structure located well below the surface.

In the past few years I've spent a good deal of time fly fishing specifically for big stripers, mostly in the kinds of waters that are the stomping grounds of live-bait and conventional-tackle fishermen. The larger fish that live in these waters are there to feed on larger baits, like squid, herring, and bunker. Here are some of the techniques that have been developed to take these fish on the fly.

Figure 95   You won't see this every day, but when you do you're in for some action. (Photo by Dave Rimmer)

Big baits must be duplicated with big flies. And big flies—like the Groceries or even bigger bunker flies—cannot be cast on light fly rods. The trick about taking fish on these flies is to first identify the correct feeding stations to cast to, and second allow your fly to sink into the strike zone depth before retrieving. In general, most presentations should be made across the current, not parallel to it. (Your first or last cast at some hot spot can defy this rule, since in the former case you have not yet drifted back to the structure, and in the latter you've gone past it.) Once you have drifted parallel to the feeding station, a cast across the current will frequently give your fly the longest exposure to the strike zone. This is certainly true of sand shoals or any structure that lies perpendicular to the current's flow.

For casting large flies into shallower water I still tend to use heavy sinking heads—I just start my retrieve the second my line hits the water. The exception to this is in darkness, or very low light, when I use a very heavy intermediate line. If I have a tangle, I don't want my fly to sink into the rocks when I can't see well enough to clear the line.

Big baitfish are strong swimmers and can really move when pursued by bass. To duplicate this panic I suggest rapid strips, completely extending your stripping arm.

Since nobody can continue this for long, however, I alternate these with slower strips, but continue to use long arm motions. A long strip with your rod pointed directly at the fly moves the fly quickly for several feet, creating the illusion that it's a large meal about to get away. The strikes are savage!

Not all big-water boat fishing is sinking-line fishing. If you fish shallow, moving water or estuaries, you will likely get plenty of shots at aggressive surface-feeding stripers. Your fly and line selection here are not usually critical, within reason. The special considerations on a boat are as follows: First, run your boat around and well uptide of the fish so that you can drift quietly into the ruckus. Second, be prepared to cast. It doesn't hurt to be trailing 15 or 20 feet of line as you approach the fish; this allows you to make a roll cast, shoot line on your backcast, and make a 60-foot or better cast with ease. Once you've placed a fly into hot fish, you can retrieve very slowly. The bass are especially willing to take the stunned or crippled victims of their attacks. Don't worry about lining aggressively feeding stripers; throw across the whole school if you can—your chances of a hookup will be that much better. You can, however, spook quietly feeding bass, especially in shallow water; you're better off to cast to the edges of these fish.

Once it's on the line, your chances of landing a large bass from the boat are better than from shore. Large bass that might get you around a rock can be lifted away from bottom snags if you apply sufficient pressure and keep the boat over them. Once the bass is close to your boat—unless the craft is absurdly high sided—you are almost at its level, and you don't need to worry about climbing around rocks or the pull of the surf. You cannot, however, simply back up and ground the fish on the shore. Because of the difficulty of handling fish near the boat, most fly rods that are broken on fish are broken at this time. Here's my own system for getting your hands near the fish without bending your rod uncomfortably (Fig. 96): When a tired bass is close to your boat, strip out a few feet of slack line, then, with your rod hand, grab the rod just toward the butt from the middle. Squeezing the line between your thumb and index finger, raise your hand over your head and point the rod directly at the fish. Reach up toward the rod tip with your line hand, and make a circle around the rod with your thumb and index finger. Slide these fingers along the rod, allowing it to bend a little if needed, until you get to the line. In one motion grasp the line beyond the rod tip with your line hand, release the line from your rod hand, and set the rod down—no pressure will be placed on the rod, because the extra line that you stripped from the reel will run through the guides. You are now handlining the fish. Just be prepared to let the line go and grab the rod should the bass make a renewed effort.

Figure 96   Landing large bass.

Step 1: The tired fish nears the angler.

Step 2: Strip out some slack line.

Step 3: Squeeze line against the rod just below midrod level.

Step 4: Point the rod at the fish.

Step 5: Make a circle with your thumb and index finger and slide it toward the rod tip.

Step 6: Tucking the rod under your arm, hold the line in your hand and release slack with the other hand.

Step 7: Hand-line the fish toward you; you can let the line go and put the fish back on the rod if necessary.

Night Fishing

Whether from boat or from shore, night fishing is the most productive way to catch stripers, especially big ones. In the cool waters of the spring or late fall, at dawn or dusk or even on stormy days, stripers may feed as actively as they usually do at night. When large, desirable baits are abundant, bass can even stage a blitz during a sunny afternoon. Typically, however, striped bass are nocturnal predators. Many people don't like night fishing: You can't see as clearly, and some spots from shore, or boat, can be downright dangerous to fish. On the other hand, for those who are comfortable enough with their tackle to fish at night, night fishing holds its own pleasures. On most nights you can see surprisingly well. Moonlight, reflected light, and the lights of civilization give your own predatory eyes enough to work with. For me the pinnacle of shore fishing—my favorite kind—is discovering large bass working visibly in the nighttime shallows of a calm back beach. Here, much like flats fishing, you are close to the bass but in a way that appeals to your nocturnal faculties.

Figure 97 Coop "The Magician" Gilkes with proof that nighttime fishing's the right time. (Photo by Pip Winslow)

Night fishing requires some special equipment, as discussed in chapter 7 (see page 82). Your most important asset will be, however, the application of the feeding-station information for shore fishing that I discussed earlier (see page 85), as well as some advance reconnaissance. While you should always wear glasses while fly fishing—even if just for eye protection—this is imperative at night. You should also be cautious about selecting the area you fish. A rambling jetty is risky enough in daylight; after dark it is a very dangerous place. Not only is it easier to fall and be injured, but in rough weather you can also be blindsided by an unseen wave. A calm sand beach poses no special threats at night, and the fish are likely to move in close after dark.

In the dark you are likely to encounter surface action on small prey species. These baitfish crowd the shorelines, secure from birds and other daytime predators.

Spearing hide in the surface film, sand eels leave their burrows to forage, and schools of "peanut bunker" swim shoulder to shoulder in the sanctuary of shoal water, all resulting in the potential for visible, and audible, feeding activity. This action will likely take the form of wakes of moving fish, the rustle of bait, or sips and pops as bait is taken from the surface. All tell you that fish are here, and are feeding.

The concentrations of bait you'll find along a nighttime shoreline make it imperative that you carefully and quietly cover the water near the beach before you cast to deeper waters. The movements of the waters, and the fish's relationships to their feeding stations, are no different at night. Only the pace has changed; it is slower. Try different retrieves, different-size flies, and different-colored flies—especially black, which silhouettes well against the night sky. Also try floating flies, slowly and hesitantly retrieved or dead drifted. Be prepared for gentle takes. Stripers don't expend the energy required for smashing strikes if they can rise casually and suck in their prey. This is what I meant earlier when I wrote of the bass's actions as pure instinct: Stripers have no honor, nor do they find any glory in the way that they take their prey. They simply use the most efficient methods available to them.

Fighting a bass at night requires no special techniques until you prepare to land the fish. If I'm into a school of small bass, I sometimes slide my fingers down my leader until I feel the hook, then—without a light—turn the fish around and unhook it. In general, however, I use a light, especially if there is any chance that it's a fish with real teeth (like a bluefish or weakfish). Turn your light on a bit in advance so that the fish swims into the light, rather than suddenly illuminating it, which could cause panic. Contrary to tradition, I have found no ill effects to my fishing from occasionally shining a light around my feet. While I wouldn't shine a light out onto feeding fish, I have used my light to unhook fish all night long without disrupting their feeding.

CHAPTER 12

Wind, Weather, and Tides

Where I grew up on the coast of Maine the old commercial fishermen were proud of their ability to foretell the weather. Indeed, their forecasts were frequently fundamentally correct, if often inaccurate as to the timing or severity of the coming conditions. Weather has always been important to all fishing, but it's much more so to the saltwater fly fisher. Of all the aspects of weather, wind force and direction, along with barometric pressure, are the most important. It may rain, and it may be cool at different times during the striper season, but since little stripering is done during the winter, you should be able to handle such conditions with the clothing that I discussed in chapter 7. Wind is another matter.

The whole upper half of the East Coast shares many of the same weather patterns. While it's a long way from Maine to North Carolina, in both locations most of the high- and low-pressure systems that make up the weather travel in an easterly or northeasterly direction. Many storms originate in the South, including the Gulf of Mexico, then come up the East Coast from Hatteras to Maine. Often, the big slow-moving high-pressure systems of the summer simply move in and engulf the entire region. It's a lot warmer in Virginia than in Massachusetts, of course, and the cool, dry Canadian highs that New England is famous for don't often make it south of

New Jersey. In general, though, the weather along the striper coast differs only in terms of degree.

Winds from the south and west are usually fair and good for fishing—but as one of my guide friends with a lot of experience says, "I don't trust anything with an N in it." I've personally done all right in light northeasterly and easterly winds, although they often foretell or accompany bad weather. My guide friend's opinion of north or northwest winds, however, is confirmed by my own experiences. These winds are frequently caused by high pressure building in, and air moving from it to a low that's departing to the east. I don't know why, but the advent of bright, clear, high-pressure weather usually sends fishing into a tailspin. Occasionally, however, especially during the fall, clear northwesterly blows can produce good fishing—probably on ravenous migrating fish.

An old mariner's rhyme, said to come from the days of the Grand Banks schooners, goes like this:

> Wind from the north, venture not forth.
> Wind from the east, fishing the least.
> Wind from the south, blows the bait into the fish's mouth.
> Wind from the west, fishing the best.

While there are frequent exceptions, and substantial ones, this rhyme is quite accurate by my experiences.

I talked earlier about why a wind blowing onto a structure improves its fishing potential. A look at the coastline, however, proves that no wind can simultaneously blow the "right" way onto all the good places. Conversely, no matter which direction the wind comes from, some structure will find it favorable for fishing.

Tide must also be taken into account—not only its stage in the high-to-low continuum but also its size relative to normal water movements. Tides are caused by the gravitational pull of primarily the moon, but also the sun, on the waters of the world. The upper East Coast of this country has some of the most consistent tides in the world. Still, a great deal of variance exists between locations, even those in the same area. The constrictive effects of the waters running through Vineyard Sound, for instance, create an almost perpetual high tide somewhere on Martha's Vineyard, even though it's only 30 miles from one end of the island to the other. The complicated effects of the moon's orbit and the earth's rotation cause each location on the coast to experience two periods in each day when its water has been drawn away (low tide), or additional water has been pushed in (high tide). As the water moves from one stage to the next, the tide is said to be running, creating the currents that make many feeding stations work. New striper anglers frequently ask, "What's the best tide?" There is, of course, no single answer. Stripers want bait to feed on, and they want conditions that make this feeding easy. Each feeding area, however, requires a different stage of the tide to provide bass with the most advantageous conditions for catching baitfish. So it can be quite complicated to analyze the interconnected effects that wind, weather, and tide have on any given piece of bass water. For example, a gentle southerly blowing onto a low-tide beach may be meaningless, because the water is too low to hold any fish. Additionally, some of the bay and river systems that stripers inhabit have reduced or even nonexistent tides. Their feeding areas may be more influenced by freshwater flowage or wind. Tides are yet another reason why newcomers to striper fishing should consult local fly shops for information. Here are some other bits of information that might help you analyze your best fishing moves in light of wind, weather, and tides.

Listen to the National Weather Service forecasts before you go on the water, and believe them. NWS marine forecasts can be found on weather radios and marine radios (VHF). In fact, it's nearly essential that a coastal fisherman own one of these radios. Even a small-boat owner should carry at least a handheld VHF. The exact timing and/or intensity of conditions may be a bit off, in NWS forecasts, but don't bet against them, either. Various sites on the Internet can also provide marine weather forecasts for the area you want to fish. One site called *marineweather.com* is particularly easy to use. Its address is http://www.marineweather.com/.

You probably can't fly fish comfortably into any wind of over 15 knots, but you may be able to work around it. In some cases I have been able to cast only 30 feet into a stiff breeze, but my boat's rapid drift pulled out all of my fly line just in time to retrieve over the structure I was targeting. Stripers like the wind; it stirs things up to their advantage. On the other hand, winds in excess of 20 knots are dangerous—even inshore—in a small boat. If a wind of even 15 knots is opposing a strong current (over 1½ knots), especially in an exposed area, it can quickly become dangerously rough. And remember that at daybreak, the wind can be deceptively calm. It's okay to fish this lull, as long as you know that if high wind is forecast, it will develop; don't put yourself in a spot you can't get out of. Before you go anywhere in a small boat, imagine what your trip back might be like when the forecast conditions arrive. I find myself fishing more frequently from the shore at both the beginning and the end of the season, since I have seen the result of playing things too close with the sea. You must think ahead and be cautious in coastal boating.

Fish with the wind in your face if you have a choice. The windward shore, all else being equal, will be the fishiest. Plan your fishing strategy in advance by sitting down with the weather forecast and a chart of the area. Keep in mind what you know of structure, the tides that will occur, and the wind direction.

Although water can definitely be moved by the wind, tides are its major influence. New and full moons bring extra-high and -low tides. These large tides increase the speed of the water moving between tide stages. Just as with the wind, so faster-moving water can increase fishing potential. These tides, however, also flush out weeds from the shoreline and leave it floating on the water's surface, which can make fishing difficult.

Bright full moons are supposed to be bad for fishing. They usually are, but I've also had some great nights under a full moon. So while I wouldn't plan a weekend trip to coincide with a full moon, it wouldn't keep me from heading out near home for a few hours, either.

Captain Dave Pecci of Bath, Maine, once gave a seminar in which he articulated the confusion I've felt for some time about barometric pressure. "I don't always know what they'll do," said Dave, "but a change in the pressure will change the fish." This change can be good or bad, depending on the pattern that's being interrupted. I've seen some dependable feeding patterns interrupted by fresh high pressure. I've also seen the dropping barometer of an incoming storm create a bass feeding blitz. On balance, though, times of change in weather patterns are great times to grab your rod and hit the shoreline.

When it comes to fishing under less-than-textbook-perfect conditions, I'm reminded of a comment made by Pat Abate, the owner of a Connecticut fly shop and a veteran of a lot of cold-weather surf casting. One afternoon in the 1980s, Pat and I were sharpening our hooks and looking out at some approaching weather that we thought might affect our upcoming night's fishing. Pat said, "I've got a new philosophy: They [the bass] can't go anywhere, they live out there, and they've got to eat every day." Through the years my business and family commitments have often kept me from arriving on the water at the perfect time and under perfect conditions. I've also done my share of hitting the alarm clock and rolling back under the covers because I thought I heard too much wind outside. I've learned, however, that if you want to catch stripers, you must fish whenever you can, and make the most of every opportunity.

If you show up to fish a beach and the water is full of weeds, or you can't get near a tide rip because it's too rough, have an alternative plan. Many times I've moved around a corner to escape unproductive conditions—and walked right into bass city. I've often prospered by pulling my hood down a little tighter and making a few more casts, or driving down the beach and trying one more spot. To some degree, we make our own luck—not only by skill but also hard work. Besides, as the saying goes, a bad day fishing is better than a great day at the office.

PART IV

Where to Do It

CHAPTER 13

Up and Down the Coast

In this chapter I present an overview of striper fishing with a fly rod in each state that holds the fish—from North Carolina up the coast to Maine. I haven't listed every spot; a whole book could be written on each state alone. My intention is simply to give you the flavor of each state's fishery, mention a few of the better spots, and offer some hints on how the locals do it. I can't stress enough how important it is that you call a local fly shop. The folks there should be very helpful—and if they're not, they deserve to have you call someone else. My list of shops is also partial—I'm sure that there are many more excellent shops to be found. I spoke with virtually all of the ones listed, though, and there's a wealth of knowledge represented there. Part of your trip planning should also include checking with the regulatory agencies that I have listed for the latest regulations.

North Carolina

North Carolina marks the southern end of the East Coast's migratory striper range—while some stripers may go farther south, the bulk of the migration seldom reaches south of Cape Point, at Hatteras. Before the mid-1970s, many large stripers wintered over along the Outer Banks from Virginia Beach south to Ocracoke Island.

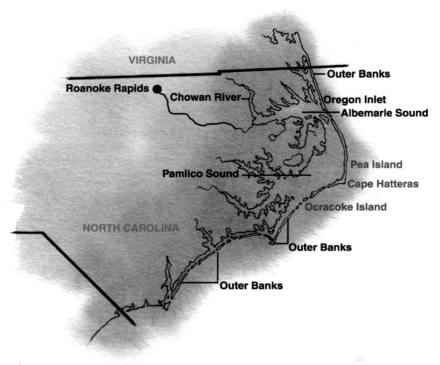

Figure 98   North Carolina.

The area off Pea Island was known to be the center of this habitat, and some truly gigantic fish were netted. With the striper crash of the 1980s, however, this fishery disappeared. Today, a winter-season striper fishery is starting to develop again on the Outer Banks, and some stripers can be found year-round in North Carolina. These are probably residents of the Roanoke River population that venture into Albemarle Sound, or out to the beaches, during the warmer months of the year. This far south stripers share the surf with many warmer-water species, and the cold-water-tolerant Chesapeake Bay stripers don't start arriving until well into

November, when the summer inhabitants are leaving. The better fishing here holds up until well into January, weather permitting—and stripers are available to diehards on warm days throughout the winter. This is especially true south of Hatteras on Ocracoke Island. There is one caveat that I must mention: North Carolina still allows ocean haul seining. In this commercial fishery, surf boats launched from the beach drag a seine out into the surf, encircle a school of fish, and drag it back to shore. Surf fishermen are regularly displaced by the seiners, who will simply set up all around recreational anglers catching fish. A friend of mine just returned from the Outer Banks vowing not to return until the haul-seine fishery was eliminated.

Because of clashes with property owners and conflicts with nesting shore-birds, places that allow beach driving are becoming rarer. North Carolina is one state that continues to allow a lot of beach-buggy access, however. In the fall you can drive along the beaches of the Outer Banks and search for working birds, especially the gannets that mean large baitfish. In 1997 one lucky group of anglers ran across a 2-mile school of breaking bass that ranged up to 40 pounds in weight. These fish were driving weakfish and menhaden high and dry onto the beach, presenting perfect fly-rod targets.

Another approach is to work the obvious structure. Places like the moving waters of Oregon and Hatteras Inlets, as well as the bar at Cape Point itself, can produce. A boat is very helpful (ramps are available), but shore fishing is also possible. In either case this is big water, and local information can be vital for catching fish—and for safety, because the Outer Banks inlets are among the most dangerous waters on the East Coast. One local shop suggests the small beach in the elbow of the Oregon inlet jetty; fish this spot with large black flies in the last two hours of darkness. You can see how important local knowledge can be—this tidbit might take you years to discover on your own.

The prime baits here are mullet, menhaden, and small weakfish. These are all robust baitfish, and for these baits and conditions I suggest at least a 9-weight rod.

Except for the April-through-June spawning season, stripers are consistently available at the bridges that lead from island to island and from the mainland to the islands. The Mann's Harbor, Baum, and Wright Memorial bridges are all several miles in length and possess numerous support structures that hold fish. While the water here is generally shallow—less than 10 feet deep, except in the channels—local anglers prefer a fast-sinking head to get near the bottom in the moving water. One local expert told me that the only fly you need is a #2/0 chartreuse Clouser. As with many bridges, casting near the supports is the key to success. These bridge fish average only 3 pounds, but individuals of 20 or more aren't uncommon. You need a boat to access these fish. In all the states that have "producer" status (those states where stripers spawn and are allowed a more liberal harvest policy on smaller striped bass), of which North Carolina is one, regulations change as you move from the ocean into the bays. Check with the authorities listed below for the latest rules.

Perhaps the jewel of North Carolina's striper fishery is the Roanoke River. Chuck Laughridge, a businessman from Roanoke Rapids, heads a group called the Roanoke Valley Striper Associ-ation. Chuck and his group have adopted a "riverkeeper" relationship with the Roanoke—a unique approach to the preservation of this fishery. Chuck's plan has been to bring prominent figures from the sporting world together with politi-cians and fisheries managers for an evening meeting, followed by a day on the river. The results have been the development of some cutting-edge con-servation measures, and an important awareness of the value of this fishery.

In late March the Roanoke's striper population ascends the river. Leaving Albemarle Sound, the stripers migrate 120 miles from the tidewaters into the totally freshwater environment of

Figure 99   Shad provide excellent nutrition for stripers spawning in Roanoke as their spawning runs coincide. (Photo by Tom Earnhardt)

Roanoke Rapids. By late April the river is literally filled with stripers; catches of over 100 fish per day are not unusual. By early May the calm of dusk finds the river for miles below the Weldon launching ramp alive with "rock fights"—the sur-face activities that take place as ripe female bass, locally called rockfish, rise to the surface surrounded by 10 or more bucks, or small male bass. The excited males bunt the sides of the cow to drive out her eggs, which they then fertilize with milt. Years ago hoop netters used one swoop to catch and kill a whole group of spawning fish; today anglers fish with a single barbless hook for a brief window of time, and may keep only a small personal-use limit. Chuck estimates that over 50 percent of these anglers use a fly rod. The Roanoke Rapids fishery holds up until June, at which time the spawned-out bass head back down to Albemarle Sound and the ocean.

The conditions of this fishery are unusual in that the river near Roanoke Rapids is shallow and filled with rocks, like a large trout stream. Shore fishing is difficult, because the silt-laden river runs through the edges of the overhanging trees at this time of year. A shallow-draft aluminum boat, ideally with jet drive, is all you need in this protected body of water. Boat anglers anchor on the edges of fast water and cast into the edges of the current with heavily weighted and brightly colored Clousers. Green fur-strips

Figure 100   A good striper from Roanoke. Note the high, silty waters. (Photo by Tom Earnhardt)

and Whistlers are also recommended by local experts. Closely mimicking a baitfish is irrelevant at this time, since these fish have more than food on their minds and are unselective. Though the water is shallow, the currents make the use of heavy sinking-tip fly lines imperative. The average fish in the Roanoke Rapids fishery is only a few pounds, but larger ones and genuine cows are present in enough numbers to keep things interesting. Be very careful while boating in rapids: It takes constant vigilance to avoid hitting the many rocks present.

Finally, a summertime fishery exists throughout Albemarle Sound and the bridges across its tributaries, like the Alligator and Chowan Rivers. Because of the many other species available in the area, and the proximity of the more popular Outer Banks, this fishery is not intensely pressured. I'm sure that fishing the open sound in low light with conventional water-reading techniques would yield some stripers. At the turn of the century a 125-pound striper, the largest ever recorded, was taken from the Chowan.

Contacts

Roanoke area: Colston's Tackle Box, 232 Highway 48, Gaston, NC 27832 (919-537-6485); Halifax County Tourisim Development Authority (1-800-522-4282).

Outer Banks: Capt. Marty's, 5151 South Croatan Highway, Nags Head, NC 27959 (1-800-627-8979).

Regulatory agency: North Carolina Division Marine Fisheries, P.O. Box 769, Morehead City, NC 28557-0769 (919-726-7021), Web page http://www.ncfisheries.net/.

Virginia

Of all the midcoast states Virginia may have the most to offer the traveling striped bass fly fisher. It holds the estuarine fisheries of the Chesapeake Bay's spawning rivers; the wide reaches of the lower bay, including the Chesapeake Bay Bridge Tunnel megastructure; and the oceanic barrier islands. Like North Carolina, bass fishing goes on year-round, and the resident stripers are joined in the autumn by the stocks migrating south from New England. Interestingly, I find the tackle shops in Virginia to be among the most enthusiastic about the quality of their fishery. One fly-shop owner told me that he could almost guarantee a visiting fly fisher a striper, even in the dead of winter. With so much good fishing available, the biggest question you must face on a visit to Virginia is what kind of fishing appeals to you most.

In late March the stripers start to ascend the major spawning rivers on the southwestern shore of the Chesapeake Bay. The James, York, Rappahannock,

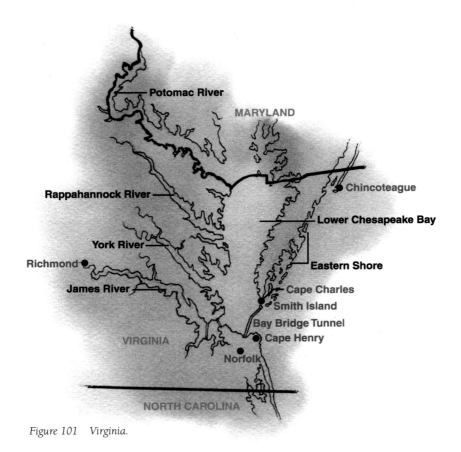

Figure 101   Virginia.

and Potomac rivers are wide, comparatively slow-flowing bodies of water that produce many of the juveniles that go on to make up the East Coast striper population. In the spring the rivers fill with spawning- and pre-spawning-age fish. Anadromous herring and shad also ascend the rivers, and make up an important forage base. Fish are caught either by casting to surface action, or by working the varied structure, including channel edges, points of land, and man-made structure such as bridges. The Benjamin Harrison Bridge near Hopewell and the Route 5 bridge over the James are both reported to be excellent; boat ramps are available. Recently, for the first time in memory, stripers have begun moving through Richmond rapids. As in the Roanoke, these fish are about 100 miles above the river's exit into the Chesapeake Bay.

Literally millions of stripers are massed in the Potomac during the spawning season, and they ascend this river all the way to the nation's capital. There is a good deal of shore access, but small-boat fishermen have a great advantage. Eight- or 9-weight rods are sufficient, along with sinking lines and chartreuse and white Clousers and Deceivers.

The biggest fish of the year are here in the springtime—in fact, many of the biggest stripers alive are present in the spawning reaches of these rivers.

Spawning fish represent a unique chance at a big striper, on the fly, in shallow water. By June these bass have gone north, although a large number of stripers that can weigh in the low teens are in year-round residence.

With the end of the spawning season, much of the action moves down to the mouths of the rivers. As the waters warm the fishing action centers on channel edges, large structure like bridges, and the mothballed navy fleet at the mouth of the James. These are definitely places for fast-sinking heads and weighted flies like Clousers.

Many of the bay's year-round stripers take up residence along the shores of the rock islands that are part of the Chesapeake Bay Bridge Tunnel. From late May through September fly fishers who cast right against the rocky, riprap structure can experience terrific action on bass of all sizes. A large white fly that imitates the bay's menhaden population is a good choice. This fishery is one of your best opportunities along the bridge tunnel.

Claude Bain, who is the recreational fishing coordinator for the commonwealth, took George Reiger and I out for a day's fishing one November around the bridge tunnel. By this time of year migrating stripers are schooling up in the mouth of the bay, near the bridge. We fished under a flock of gulls, from which George, a noted conservation

Figure 102   The author (left) and Claude Bain caught a 34-inch Chesapeake striper near Bay Bridge Tunnel. (Photo by George Reiger)

of the barrier islands of the Eastern Shore peninsula can often find migrating schools of stripers of all sizes. These islands are largely in the hands of conservation organizations, and are without land access. Beach driving is not possible, although boat-launching ramps are common throughout the area. The ocean beach fishing continues on the south side of the Chesapeake Bay. Sand Bridge Beach, just south of Virginia Beach, is especially known for stripers. No vehicle access is allowed, but excellent fishing is available, especially at night near the pilings of the pier. Toward the bridge a number of tide rips appear as the bay empties on a dropping tide. The area between the green can and Cape Henry has a rip that produces many large stripers.

writer, identified five separate species. The flock was approximately 2 miles long by $\frac{1}{4}$ mile wide, and bass were scattered throughout the area that the birds were reconnoitering. Every few casts drew a strike from the fattest schoolies I can remember seeing. Later that morning we drifted along a flat about halfway across the bay, where I picked a 34-inch bass by blind casting with a 550-grain Superhead and a yellow Groceries. (You should also have at least a 9-weight, and preferably a 10- or 11-weight, for this kind of fishing.) Claude, who spends 200-plus days a year in his "floating office," thought it was a ho-hum day. Later in November and even into December schools of very large stripers work the surface in this area, especially around the Smith Island flats to the east, on the north end of the bridge.

In fact, similar to North Carolina, anglers running a boat along the outside

Shorebound anglers can also enjoy success along Chesapeake Beach, which stretches from right under the bay bridge tunnel (a great spot to try) all the way down to Cape Henry. Local fly shops report good access. As with any of the areas that I have listed, I strongly suggest you check in with a local fly shop and even hire a guide, at least to start, if your pocketbook can handle it. In the lower bay and ocean areas there is a profusion of larger baitfish, especially during the fall season. Menhaden, which are iffy in the North, are common here in all size ranges, as are mullet and large spearing. The bay is a nursery area for many species, and in the fall the migrating bass also feed on the half-grown young of such species as spot, croaker, and weakfish. This means you should offer good-size flies. White Deceivers and chartreuse Clousers are popular patterns. One local shop suggests tying Clousers with oversize aluminum eyes to give the appearance of a larger baitfish. I like throwing a fly that seems large enough to attract a big fish.

Contacts

Inner bay: Kruse's Wharf, H.C.R. 01, Box 442, Deltaville, VA 23043 (804-776-6200); Sandy Point Bait & Tackle, 5015 Colley Avenue, Norfolk, VA 22473 (757-440-7696).

Outer bay and ocean: Angler's Lab Outfitters, 1554 Laskin Road, Virginia Beach, VA 23451 (757-491-2988).

Western Shore rivers: Pony Pasture Fly & Tackle, 7045 Forest Hill Avenue, Richmond, VA 23225 (804-272-8070).

Regulatory agency: Virginia Marine Resources Commission, 2600 Washington Avenue, Box 756, Newport News, VA 23607 (757-247-2200), Web page http://www.state.va.us/mrc/.

Maryland

Maryland has a reputation as the official home of the striped bass. While the state splits the Chesapeake Bay habitat with Virginia, some of the striper's most prolific grounds are the upper bay around the Susquehanna River, and famed Eastern Shore rivers like the Choptank and Nanticoke. Even the mention of these names commands reverence from most hard-core striper fanatics. And all of these important fishing areas are located within Maryland's boundaries.

Fly fishing for stripers has taken a strong hold in the upper bay. This area starts at Kent Narrows, where local fly-shop personnel told me that excellent shore and boat access is available. Kent Narrows gets the nod for shore fishing: The two leading fly shops in the area both independently rated it number one. While there are many other places where, assuming a little local knowledge, you can take stripers from the shore, boat anglers have a decided advantage. The upper bay is a vast

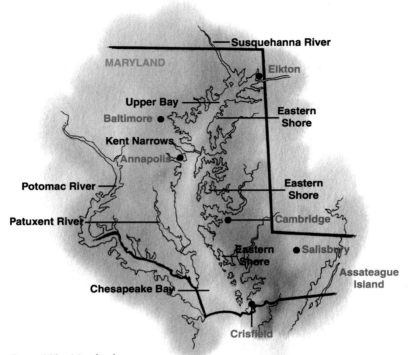

Figure 103   Maryland.

stretch of predominantly shallow and brackish water cut by winding channels and structured with shell bars along the bottom. Everything you've learned about working structure will help prepare you for fishing this large body of water.

Reading the water aside, in the late spring and early summer there are so many stripers in the upper bay that you should find plenty of surface-feeding action under working birds. Virtually all of this area is spawning habitat for stripers, and they are here in sizes from 6 ounces to 60 pounds. In the spring stripers move into the bay following the

runs of alewives, blueback herring, and shad. These fatty baitfish nourish the spawning bass and give you an opportunity to fish big flies for big stripers. A long white Deceiver will do the trick nicely. I also like yellow in turbid, brackish water like this. Later in the summer this area is filled with spearing and grass shrimp.

One of the upper bay's most important features is the mighty Susquehanna River, which is as shallow as it is broad. This provides a great opportunity for wade fishing, and it's possible for you to hook very large fish in shallow water here. My local sources of information bubble over with enthusiasm for the quality of the spring fishery on the Susquehanna. You can also fish the river from a boat but, depending on the flow from the Conowingo Dam, a spare prop is a good idea. The large anadromous baitfish of the upper bay also spawn in the Susquehanna; in fact, the river has a gigantic run of shad, which you can catch on the fly. Beware of the potential for rapidly rising waters when water is released at the Conowingo Dam, however.

To the east of the Susquehanna the upper bay becomes the Elk River, and finally the C&D Canal, which connects the Chesapeake and Delaware bays. The entrances to the canal and the area around Turkey Point Lighthouse are prime, especially from April to June. There is good public access to these areas, especially at Elk Neck State Park.

Another part of the upper bay fishery worth noting is the area around the Chester—a broad river with numerous bays and creeks. An old hand at fishing the bay told me, "Pay attention to three things: points, drop-offs, and creek mouths." Sounds familiar, but you won't even need to do this if you find surface action under birds in the springtime.

The broad, shallow expanses of the upper bay heat up dramatically in the summer. This has several ramifications for the striper fishing. First, the spawning fish leave for the coast, and the number and size of available bass diminishes greatly. Second, the large baitfish, finished with their spawning, also leave. In their place bass forage on smaller baits like spearing, grass shrimp, bay anchovies (locally called rain bait), eels, and crabs. (One local expert ties a crab-colored Clouser on a #4 hook for this summer fishing. This is about as small a fly as I have heard of being regularly used on stripers.) Later in the summer juvenile menhaden, herring, and shad are also available. Third, the bass become very nocturnal, relegating most of your fishing to dawn, dusk, or nighttime; the length of time during which bass actively feed is also reduced. In short, the heat of summer is not the best time of year to fish the upper bay. Finally, the warm brackish waters of the upper bay are low in dissolved oxygen at this time of year, making it far more difficult to successfully release stripers. You might be better off targeting other species during the summer on upper bay waters.

The middle and lower sections of the bay are made up of famous striper spawning rivers and innumerable creeks and marshes. This vast nursery ground holds the resident and premigratory stripers that are the future of the coastal fishery. Working the draining flats, marsh creek openings, points, bars, and cut banks from a small boat provides many excellent opportunities for catching smaller stripers on flies. Joe Bruce of the Fishermen's Edge in Baltimore specializes in fishing this kind of water with tackle like a 4- or 5-weight fly rod. (Trout-weight equipment like this is fairly common in New England, but rare in the mid-Atlantic.) Using the butt of such a rod you can quickly land these stripers—which means a negligible increase in mortality compared to using the heavier-weight outfits that take much of the fun out of it. The area around Baltimore Harbor is another spot where Joe has helped popularize lightweight fly fishing for stripers. Baltimore Harbor is a bit deeper than its surrounding waters, and therefore offers a more attractive environment, especially during the summer.

The lower end of Maryland's famous Eastern Shore is Tangier Sound. Here during the spring and fall at places like Holland and Kedges Straits, surface action is frequently dependable. In good years, multiple-square-mile schools of stripers feed on the surface, betrayed by tens of thousands of screaming birds. Larger bass are frequently taken on a submerged structure known as the target ship.

Finally, Maryland features a small section of ocean fishing on the east side of the Delmarva Peninsula. This whole section of shoreline, from the Chesapeake Bay Bridge Tunnel north into Delaware Bay, is largely undeveloped—including its potential for saltwater fly fishing. The fly-shop personnel I talked with said that Chincoteague Bay is filled with stripers—fishing safaris they had taken there had been very successful, but almost no one else was around. Also, Assateague Island can be driven by beach buggies with a permit; you can drive for miles along this unspoiled beach looking for birds working over fish, or reconnoitering the low-tide formations and returning at high tide to fish such structure. There are so many other fish species using the beach during the warmer months that those targeting stripers should catch the spring and fall migrations.

The inlet at Ocean City and the bridges connecting this area to the mainland are both excellent places to find stripers throughout the season, as is Assawoman Bay.

Contacts

Upper bay: Tolgate Tackle Shop, 114 North Tolgate Road, Bel Air, MD 21014 (410-836-9262); Anglers, 1456 Whitehall Road, Annapolis, MD 21401 (410-974-4013).

Western Shore: Fishermen's Edge, 1719$\frac{1}{2}$ Edmonson Avenue, Baltimore, MD 21228 (410-719-7999).

Eastern Shore: Salisbury Fly Shop, 325 Snow Hill Road, Salisbury, MD 21804 (410-543-8359).

Regulatory agency: Maryland Department of Natural Resources Fisheries Administration, Tawes State Office Building B-2, 580 Taylor Avenue, Annapolis, MD 21401 (410-260-8251), Web page http://www.dnr.state.md.us/.

Delaware

Delaware is another sleeper area for striper fly fishing. A bright-sounding young man whom I spoke with in one shop described Delaware's shoreline as "farmland and small, failed industrial towns where there just aren't many people." He also said that the place is lousy with fish. There are really two fisheries in Delaware: the ocean and the bay. Delaware Bay, the mouth of the Delaware River, is a very fishy place—yet just as on the New Jersey side, fly fishing has yet to take off on the Delaware side of the bay. In fact, according to the closest fly shops the area is lightly fished, period. A quick look at the shoreline, however, reveals at least a dozen good-size inlets along the bay shore, and I'm told that there is considerable public access to much of the area. The Delaware River has a rapidly growing population of spawning stripers, as well as receiving many migrants from the South. I'm confident that from April through October or later, an angler who applies the lessons of this book to the inlets, shoreline points, and obvious bottom structure will do very well along this shore.

Fly fishing on the ocean side appears to be much better organized. There are two key inlets here: Roosevelt Inlet, which is actually just inside the bay, provides excellent striped bass

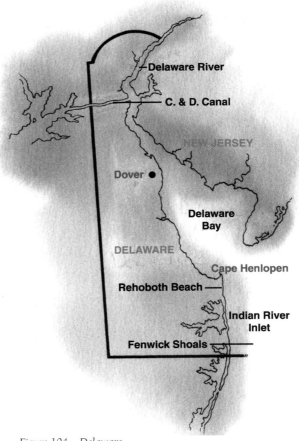

Figure 104   Delaware.

angling and boating access, and Indian River Inlet, a well-known fishing location. The latter inlet plays host to stripers all season, but the fishing really improves during the fall migration in October and November. Additionally, beach buggies are allowed on almost all of Delaware's beaches. From around September 15 to October 15, a run of mullet along the beaches can provide some awesome fishing. A large white Deceiver or a Groceries should successfully mimic these baitfish. The area around Fenwick Shoals, about 10 miles north of Ocean City, Maryland, can be a key location for boaters during the entire fall.

Indian River and Rehoboth bays also provide excellent fly fishing. A canal connects Roosevelt Inlet with Rehoboth Bay, and its exits and entrances are fine locations for stripers. The fish are present in good numbers during the summer, but become very fussy when feeding on small bait back in the bays. Bay anchovies and spearing are the most common. Nighttime offers the best summer action.

A rip develops just off Cape Henlopen that can be very productive. And right on shore and just west of this point lies a large, unnamed tidal flat. The water leaving the bay moves gently across this flat, the bottom of which varies in depth from 2 to 8 feet. This flat is very wadable and, according to the local experts, offers some of the state's premier fly fishing for stripers of all sizes.

Contacts

Captain Mac's, Route 54, Fenwick, DE (302-436-2445).

Regulatory agency: Department of Natural Resources and Environmental Control, Division of Fish and Wildlife, 89 King's Highway, Dover, DE 19903 (302-739-5296), Web page http://www.dnrec.state.de.us/.

Pennsylvania

Pennsylvania may seem an unlikely state to include in a discussion of striped bass fishing—indeed, this is the first book I know of to do so—but I do so with very good reason. As recently as the 1970s, the Delaware was a river in tough shape. In the summer, a large block of water without sufficient oxygen for fish life existed in the greater Philadelphia area. Pollution-abatement measures of various kinds have changed all that, however, and the remnant spawning population of stripers has again become robust. This rejuvenated stock has created, as it has on the Roanoke, an entirely new fishery.

Figure 105   Pennsylvania.

In May stripers pour in from Delaware Bay and spawn in the river between the Philadelphia airport and the Delaware Memorial Bridge. Fly angling for these fish, just as in Delaware Bay, has not yet developed to anywhere near its potential. I spoke with people at a number of shops in the Philadelphia area, and they gave me only excuses as to why almost no one fly fishes for stripers in the lower river. As an old river fisherman, I found them all weak. Working the structure or looking for birds working over feeding fish in the Delaware's spawning reaches during May and June has to pay off—big time! Above Trenton, New Jersey, oddly

enough, is where most action is currently taking place.

Starting around Memorial Day, as spawning is coming to a close, many stripers move up the river for the summer rather than out to the bay. These bass are taken all the way to Bushkill, beyond the Delaware Water Gap, where the river is crossed by the Appalachian Trail—over 120 miles from the sea. (This also happens to some degree with several other riverine striper spawning populations—the Hudson is another example.) Here the river is entirely fresh and nontidal. The Delaware sports a large run of anadromous fish, including shad and blueback herring. Stripers feed aggressively on both as they move up to spawn and fall back to the ocean. In the early fall the bass lie in the downstream currents like giant brown trout, feeding on the millions of young herring dropping back down to the ocean. Between these times the stripers forage on all the normal freshwater life, including eels and freshwater minnows. Stripers in this environment become very nocturnal. Once water temperatures start to climb, the summer fishing—other than at dusk, dawn, and the middle of the night—is slow.

These are not all school bass, either. Stripers of 20 or more pounds are far from uncommon. The average is, however, 5 or 6 pounds. What other freshwater river fishery can you think of with fish that compare?

Additionally, as if designed to please the fly angler, the fishing is almost entirely wade. A canoe or small boat is helpful mostly to get you from spot to spot. Be careful, however: This river is full of rocks, and there are extended stretches of nonnavigable rapids.

According to one local expert a white Deceiver is the only fly necessary. "You can catch them on a lot of different flies," said the expert, "but you only need a white Deceiver." Your bigger trout tackle or salmon rod will do fine—you are fishing trout water.

By the end of September this fishery is drawing to a close. The shallow river cools quickly, and the stripers are compelled to follow the schools of immature anadromous baitfish down to the ocean.

Contacts

Angler's Pro Shop, 3361 Bethlehem Pike, Souderton, PA 18964 (215-721-4909), e-mail anglerspro@enter.net, Web page www.flyfishers.com/anglers-pro.

Regulatory agency: Pennsylvania Fish and Boat Commission, P.O. Box 67000, Harrisburg, PA 17106-7000 (717-657-4515), Web page http://www.state.pa.us/PA_Exec/Fish_Boat/pfbchom2.html.

New Jersey

When it comes to striped bass fly fishing, New Jersey is a state with a lot going on. To begin with, all of the great things I said about the upriver fishery in Pennsylvania apply equally to New Jersey, which owns the other bank of the river. And in Delaware Bay, you'll find the same conditions that exist on its Delaware side. There are tons of fish. In a 1997 seine haul designed to measure the striper population made just north of Cape May by the New Jersey fisheries people, a mind-boggling quantity of stripers came ashore. Still, try as I might, I could find no shop that catered to fly fishers in this area. Cape May is an old commercial port, and an active charter fleet works the rips off the cape with conventional tackle. Again, I'm certain that the techniques I've discussed in this book will bring a lot of fly-rod stripers to hand. And in contrast to much of the rest of New Jersey, you probably won't be too crowded.

Turning the corner at Cape May we head north along a stretch of beach that doesn't change much until the mouth of the Hudson, at Sandy Hook. This is the famous Jersey Shore. When Van Campen Heilner wrote about it, the Jersey barrier beaches were still wild. But the fish can't see all the recent development, and the fishing is still first rate. In some areas the aesthetics aren't bad, either, since some of the barrier islands are in the hands of conservation groups. New Jersey's long history of sportfishing and dense population have combined to create some significant benefits for the striped bass.

I can't talk about stripers and New Jersey without mentioning Tom Fote.

Figure 106   New Jersey.

Tom spent years on the Atlantic States Marine Fisheries Commission fighting for the rights of personal-use anglers. After striper populations collapsed Tom and the Jersey Coast Anglers Association—the advocacy arm of New Jersey's fishing clubs—championed legislation that prohibited commercial fishing for stripers in that state. He also sees to it that a bill is introduced in every session of Congress that will give the striper the same protection on a federal level. While we aren't there yet, Tom's efforts have done more than any other individual's to make fisheries managers aware of the importance of stripers to the fishing public.

New Jersey also has a long history of fishing with the saltwater fly rod. It was in the late 1950s that Joe Brooks, Lefty Kreh, Mark Sosin, and other notables joined with local fly-fishing fanatics at the late Cap Colvin's luncheonette to form the Saltwater Fly Rodders of America. In the early 1970s the club broke up and sent its records to the IGFA. Many of its members have gone on to become either professional personalities in the fly-fishing industry or innovators who spread the word about the possibilities and pleasures of fishing the ocean with a fly rod. My friend John DeFilippis is the president of its resurrection as the Atlantic Saltwater Fly-Rodders of America. In the old tradition this group started out tying flies at the house of Bob Popovics, credited with inventing epoxy flies, and has now built its membership to nearly 300.

The old building that once housed Colvin's place still exists outside the entrance to Island Beach State Park. And while changes in tackle distribution have eliminated some of the half-dozen shops that formerly stood outside the park's gates, there are still several almost in a row. On a cold Saturday morning in late November you must stand in line even at 6 A.M. to get a seat in the diner section of Betty and Nick's tackle shop. Without a doubt, the Jersey Shore has the most active saltwater fly-rod fishing culture to be found on the East Coast.

Fishing along this long stretch of beach starts in early April, when the shallow bays in back of the beach begin quickly to warm. By the first of May stripers of all sizes are moving along the beaches as the bunker migration moves up the coast. During the summer the water temperatures rise to the point where all the fishing action takes place after dark. From late October on until early January, waves of stripers migrate down the beach. There are huge numbers of fish present at this time, especially since New Jersey receives wintering stripers from the Hudson as well as late migrants heading for the Chesapeake Bay. Many of these fish simply spend the winter off the beach, in the channels of the inlets. Along the beaches south of here, in good fall weather, boat fishers need only cruise along looking for birds working over the schools of migrating stripers.

Stripers are caught daily at hundreds of locations along the shore, and the local fly shops can point you to places that might produce. The most dependable areas, however, are the inlets, of which there are about a dozen along the shore's span. The shorelines along the numerous islands in back of both Barnegat and Brigantine inlets are hot spots all summer long. New Jersey's coast has nearly every baitfish imaginable: herring, bunker, and squid in the spring, and mullet, sand eels, spearing, bay anchovies, and juvenile bunker and herring in the fall. A boat is necessary to get the most out of this fishing, but shore access is available here and there.

One top location for shore access is undoubtedly Island Beach State Park. The state thinks highly enough of this spot to have located the governor's mansion here, and it's easy to see why. As you roll through the gates of the park, you also travel from modern built-up New Jersey back in time to a place that Heilner would have recognized. A beach-buggy association has secured access to over 10 miles of beach running all the way back to Barnegat Inlet. You can drive along the beach working structure or looking for breaking fish. You can also fish the long jetties at the entrance to Barnegat Bay, where some huge fish are taken every year. A long straight road back through the park also provides plenty of access to the bay. Wade fishermen work this shore on summer nights taking stripers on thinly tied Deceivers or floating spearing imitations. An 8-weight for the back bay, and a 9- or 10-weight out front on the beach, with an optional floating intermediate line will work fine.

Continuing up the coast we come to the end of the barrier beach and, finally, to Sandy Hook. The beaches change after the barrier beach ends; this is due to the presence of many jetties, which provide excellent structure. Also, sand pumped onto the beach from offshore to combat erosion has created new fish-holding bars and points. The fly-shop personnel I talked with in Red Bank were big proponents of shooting heads. They rigged either a floating or an intermediate head to a braided-mono running line by using loop-to-loop braided-mono connectors. The extra distance available from this setup (braided mono shoots like a rocket) can be helpful in many shore-fishing situations.

Sandy Hook itself is a national park. A 10-mile-long access road runs almost to the tip, and numerous access points exist leading to the waters on both sides of the park. At the end of the hook a 15-minute walk leads you to a tide rip that runs right to the beach. The man I spoke with at the fly shop about this rip could barely contain his enthusiasm: "They're there now, hell, they're there all winter. You can't beat that place. It's full of bass. Yes, and big ones, too. The rip just keeps bringing the bait right on shore." I was slumped in a big chair, looking out my window at a frozen Maine landscape, as our conversation began; by the end I was on my feet ready to head out to the barn and pack my truck for a trip to this rip. One of the other features of the Sandy Hook–Raritan Bay area is a big early run of bunker that shows up around the first of May and hangs around, holding big bass, until Thanksgiving. Boaters fish an area off Sandy Hook called the triangle, which includes Romer Shoals and holds big bass in its tide rips. Heavy sinking heads and bunker flies will undoubtedly produce big fish. This whole area is really part of the mouth of the Hudson, one of the East Coast's major drainages and one that has a large spawning population of stripers.

The beaches along the Keyport area, west of the hook on Raritan Bay, have superb bassing. The warm waters of this bay host large quantities of bait chased by migratory stripers from both the Chesapeake and the Hudson's own stock. The hot fly for the whole area is a Half-and-Half, which combines a lead-eyed Clouser head with a Deceiver body. Chartreuse and white are the preferred colors. Locals also like a spun deer-hair slider for night fishing, when spearing are the bait of record.

Finally, many people forget that one entire side of the New York Harbor is in New Jersey. I haven't heard a lot about fly fishing throughout this stretch, perhaps because of the aesthetics. What I do hear, however, is that the few people who fish from boats in this area, and who worked structure like the pilings of the multitude of old docks and the tide lines around the Hudson's mouth, catch lots of bass. This fishing is, except for its backdrop, much like that in some of Maine's rivers. Super-head lines and Clousers or herring imitations in yellow are bound to work for the student of structure. Fishing can go on until well after New Year's, since these fish don't leave—they just go dormant for the winter. And every striper, big and small, along with the millions of herring that ascend the Hudson, has to run this gauntlet to get to the spawning areas upriver.

Contacts

Jersey Shore: The Fly Hatch, 90 Broad Street, Red Bank, NJ 07701 (732-530-6784), Web page http://www.flyhatch.com/; Betty and Nick's, 807 Southwest Central Avenue, Seaside Park, NJ (732-793-2708), e-mail cobra76@vitinc.com.

The Hudson: Ramsey's Sporting Goods—locations in Ramsey, Paramus, and Ledgewood, NJ (Paramus 201-261-5000).

Regulatory agency: New Jersey Division of Fish, Game and Wildlife, 501 East State Street, CN400, Trenton, NJ 08625-0400 (609-292-9410), Web page http://www.state.nj.us/dep/index.html.

New York

Like Virginia, New York has an excellent, large, and varied striper fishery. Unlike anywhere in the South, however, New York already has a vibrant, saltwater fly-rod community. Two clubs, with a combined membership of over 1000, exist on Long Island alone. Most of this has sprung up in just the last six or eight years. Another similarity is that both Virginia and New York have large spawning populations of stripers. The Hudson's exact contribution to the East Coast, especially the New England and Long Island Sound, striper fisheries is unmeasured, but it must be enormous. Once greatly depressed, the Hudson's fishery rebounded off the charts once commercial fishing there was abolished—which happened because the government found chemical pollution in the flesh of stripers.

I remember reading back in the 1970s that the center of striper spawning was thought to be near West Point. Almost no one had ever seen the stripers in the act; it was thought to happen at night. Today, because of the expanded striper population, fish spawn along the upper river all the way to the Catskills. Many people have now seen truly colossal schools of spawning stripers turning the water white in a giant northern version of a rock fight. Even more are angling for the amazing numbers of fish schooled up in the river waiting for the right moment to spawn. The center of

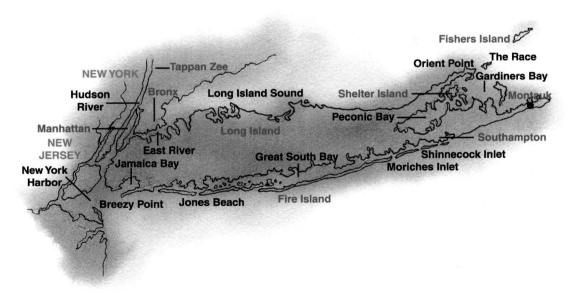

Figure 107   New York.

this activity, which takes place around the middle of May, is an area between Newburgh and Catskill. Fish of 40, 50, and 60 pounds are taken annually. Most of the action to date has been bait fishing. Some fly fishers, however, are on top of it. Since only one fish can be taken per day, and the fish are known to contain PCBs, this is largely a catch-and-release fishery. The stripers feed predominantly on herring. Sinking lines and large yellow Groceries should produce well in this silty water. This is largely a boat-fishing area, but since it's 60 to 100 miles above the ocean, the river is very manageable in a small boat. Looking for surface-feeding fish is one way to locate them; sometimes a whole school will simply rise to the surface. The river, however, has many features, including current rips, bottom lumps, points, and entering creeks, that hold fish. By later in June these fish are mostly gone, and the river becomes a warm, freshwater fishery. The Hudson spawning run is destined to become (at least in part) an important fly-rod catch-and-release fishery.

Long Island's shoreline, which runs about 120 miles from west to east, comprises most of New York's coast. Atlantic beaches run along almost the entire south side of the island. While these are the beaches of John Cole's *Striper* and hold plenty of bass, they often have a heavy ocean surge that makes fly fishing tough. Still, it can be done—and is, especially between Moriches and Shinnecock inlets, where the fall of 1997 was an excellent season for fish as large as the mid-30-inch range. Generally the inlets all along the south side are your best bet, although Breezy Point, at the mouth of Jamaica Bay, is a famous fall shore-fishing spot right next to New York City. The barrier islands that these beaches connect are largely public parklands, creating excellent access to the back beaches all along the south side. In addition, the bays between the beaches and ocean provide excellent action starting in late April, because their shallow waters warm quickly. Sand eels, spearing, and bunker are the most important baits along this shore.

The north side of the island is just as fishy and provides excellent opportunities for fly rodding. The earliest fishing starts in April between the Throgs Neck Bridge at the mouth of the East River and Stony Brook, about a third of the way out onto the island. The early fishing is on small sand eels and spearing, and is best accomplished with slim, sparse designs (locals like epoxy flies or Clousers) down to #2 in size. While predominantly small fish are taken, specimens of over 30 inches aren't uncommon. As the water warms, the bait and bass get rapidly larger and the action extends farther down the island. By the middle of May large stripers—

perhaps spawned-out breeders from the river—are moving down Long Island Sound. In the summer, bunker are in residence in many of the bays on this side of the island, and casting a large bunker pattern into a menhaden school will sometimes take a surprisingly large striper. At the end of the month a squid run develops at the east end of Long Island that accounts for many big stripers. The waters off this east end are full of tide rips created by water entering and exiting the sound. The Race, a fast-running, treacherous piece of water, has umpteen holding areas for stripers, including the waters off Plum and Fishers islands, both famous for big fish. (My personal-best fly-rod striper, one of 46 inches, came from Fishers Island's rocky shores.) Sandwiched between Long Island's north and south forks is Gardiners Bay, where in the early summer some large stripers have been taken in just 2 feet of water by sight-casting fly fishers. Farther inside the forks, a large piece of Shelter Island is in the hands of conservation groups and offers excellent fishing—as do the Peconic Bays, which stretch back to the beginning of the forks. These bays house incredible bait, including every baitfish I mentioned earlier in this book and more. This isn't crashing surf so small flies, along with either intermediate or floating lines, will typically do the job from the shore. Boat fishermen are better off with a moder-

ate-size Superhead—no larger than 350 grains.

In the fall Montauk Point becomes the center of the striper-fishing universe. Sporadically, the bunker that have spent the summer inside the sound head around Montauk Point on their way south. Big bass often are hot on their heels. In early October a run of bay anchovies starts in the sound. When the bass rise to the surface feeding on the anchovies—so tightly balled that the water turns brown—the action is heart stopping. You need a boat to best access this fishery, though the persistent angler can take them from shore. I like to throw a big Groceries on a weighted line into the ruckus, let it sink for 10 feet, then strip in long pulls. You'll catch much bigger fish this way than those trying to duplicate the inch-long bait. The last hurrah for the Northeast is a run of Atlantic herring that pulls into Montauk in mid-November. This is the fishery dreamed of all year long, the time when record bass are available from boat or shore. Turtle Cove just south of Montauk Lighthouse, and the beach that runs from just east of Lake Montauk toward Shagwong, are top fly-rod locations. You can walk to the former from its parking area, and with proper stickers you can drive along the latter beach in a four-wheel-drive vehicle.

Some excellent striper fishing is also available in one of America's most populous areas: The north shore of Long Island Sound, including the Bronx, the Westchester shoreline, and the waters of the East River, produces very well at both ends of the season. The East River connects New York Harbor and Long Island Sound, and stripers of all sizes pass this way as they exit the river in the spring and return in the fall. Fishing can start in March and last until December. During the summer an oxygen block sometimes develops in this heavily developed area. Shoreline access is limited, but Roosevelt Park does provide access to the East River, and Orchard Beach Park in the Bronx is said to be an excellent fishing location. A small boat can really expand your horizons in this area. Casting bunker patterns around structure in May and June can produce some monster bass.

Contacts

Montauk area: Dixon's Sporting Life, 74 Montauk Highway, East Hampton, NY 11937 (516-324-7979).

Long Island's north shore: Cold Spring Harbor Fly Shop, 37 Main Street, Cold Spring Harbor, NY 11724 (516-673-8937); Camp-Site Sport Shop, 1877 New York Avenue, Huntington Station, NY 11746 (516-271-4969), e-mail camp-site@juno.com.

Manhattan: Manhattan Custom Tackle, 913 Broadway, New York, NY 10010 (212-505-6690).

Hudson: Don's Tackle Service, 69 South Broadway, Red Hook, NY 12571 (914-758-9203); Hudson Valley Angler Supply, 31 Burd Street, Nyack, NY (914-353-9280).

Regulatory agency: New York State DEC, Marine Resources, 205 Belle Meade Road, East Sautauket, NY 11733 (516-444-0433), Web page http://unix2.nysed.gov/ils/executive/encon/encon.htm.

Connecticut

All of Connecticut's shoreline fronts on Long Island Sound. On a reasonably clear day the New York shoreline is visible from anywhere on the Connecticut side. This creates a somewhat unique fishing environment. First, there is no real crashing surf; second, a lot of fast-moving water travels the sound's shoreline. Also, relatively deep water is close to shore—a particularly attractive situation for saltwater fly rodders. And saltwater fly rodding for stripers is very

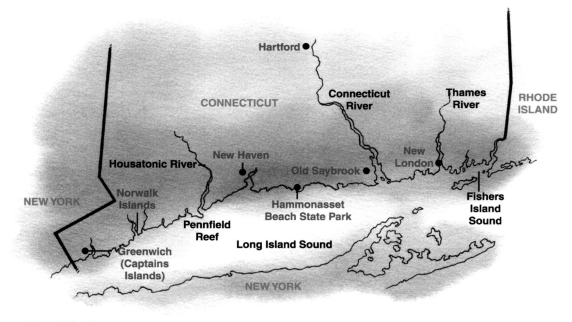

Figure 108   Connecticut.

popular in this state. You might go a while between encounters with other fly fishers in areas to the south, but not in Connecticut. In fact, in many good locations along the Connecticut shoreline there are more people fishing with fly rods than any other kind of tackle. Nor are fly casters Johnny-come-latelies in Connecticut's tidewaters. The Connecticut Saltwater Fly-Rodders, which started in 1968 as a chapter of New Jersey's Saltwater Fly Rodders of America, still meets monthly and has nearly 200 members. As a result many, if not most, area tackle shops cater to fly fishers. Provided for by both the Hudson and the Chesapeake, Connecticut has a long season in which stripers of all sizes are abundant.

The shoreline of Long Island Sound is the terminus for a number of good-size freshwater rivers, including the Hudson, via the East River; the very important Connecticut River; and the Thames. While state fisheries officials have never officially confirmed it, the presence of tiny stripers in the Connecticut almost guarantees that this river, a huge supplier of herring and shad, also has a spawning population of stripers. This and numerous smaller waterways support large populations of anadromous baitfish, which initiate the spring fishing for larger stripers. And the mainland shore experiences similar runs of baitfish, which appear at essentially the same times as reported for Long Island.

The squid run in late May generates a lot of larger fish in the Connecticut side of the Race, and in Fishers Island Sound. Later, in the fall, bay anchovy schools become numerous. Historically, bunker were an important forage; they were present throughout the sound during the summer. Recent years have seen a dearth of these big oily baitfish, except in the far western sound. The predominant baits during the summer are now spearing and sand eels, the thin imitations of which are easy to cast. Because of this small-bait fishery, Connecticut fly tyers have developed many innovative and attractive flies with slim profiles.

Starting in the western part of the sound, the biggest problem facing shorebound anglers is access. Connecticut is a prosperous and populous state; as a result the shoreline is quite private. Even boating access is difficult. Still, there is access; you just have to scratch a little. There is a state ramp in Saugatuck, and the town of Norwalk still sells some launch permits for its facility. Off the coast of Greenwich lie the Big and Little Captains Islands. The tide rips over a sand shoal between them, producing excellent striper fishing. Farther east, in Fairfield, a public right-of-way provides access to Pennfield Reef. The rocky reef bares at low water and is wadable out to its current-swept end, in the sound. One of the premier shore-fishing locations is Milford Point. It's nicknamed the bird

sanctuary, since it is owned by the Audubon Society; a key to the gate is available to members. This large area encompasses a variety of habitats, including the mouth of the Housatonic River. The Norwalk Islands, especially the western end of Sheffield Island, are productive for boaters.

In recent years an excellent striper fishery has developed in the freshwater section of the Connecticut River. While school fish predominate, some very large bass follow the herring and shad into the river in May. During May and June, stripers are taken here and there throughout the upper river, especially around the breached remains of the Enfield Dam. Clousers and Deceivers, especially in yellow or chartreuse, are effective in the turbid water.

East of New Haven, Connecticut becomes a little less developed. Shore access, while not abundant, is available if you check with the local fly shops. The large marshy areas surrounding Stony Creek are excellent, and can be fished by foot or canoe. Some excellent beach fishing is also available to the public at Harkness Memorial State Park. (There are also a few fishable state parks east of New Haven.) One local expert told me that some of eastern Connecticut's best fishing could be found at the myriad creeks, trestles, and pond openings all along the railroad's shoreline route. The other piece of wisdom that he passed on was the need to fish a bit deeper in the water column. Even if the water isn't terribly deep, using something like a Superhead or sinking-tip line will likely be several times more effective for you than floating lines in these outlets. Yellow is a favorite color. You can't beat local fly shops for this kind of detail!

Boaters in eastern Connecticut have a lot to choose from: The movement of the sound and the rocky shoreline provide many classic feeding stations. Barletts Reef, as well as the mouths of the Connecticut and Thames rivers, provides excellent opportunities. The marshy lower end of the Connecticut is full of stripers of nearly all sizes in May and June. A big launching ramp right under the Interstate 95 bridge provides excellent access.

An unusual fishery is available during the winter in the Thames River. For reasons known to no one, stripers overwinter near the head-of-tide in the Thames. Sinking-line fishermen can catch bass from a boat or the shore in the vicinity of the I-95 bridge over the river. In warm winters the action can spread downstream for a mile or two, and fish are also taken at the head of navigable water in downtown Norwich. When the weather warms in the spring, these fish leave and are replaced by fresh migrant schoolies. No spawning appears to take place—these fish are just looking for a good place to wait out the winter.

Contacts

Stratford Bait and Tackle, 1076 Stratford Avenue, Stratford, CT 06479 (203-377-8091); Hartford Club Sports, 554 Weathersfield Avenue, Hartford, CT 06114 (860-296-0110); Rivers End Tackle Company, 141 Boston Post Road, Old Saybrook, CT 06475 (860-388-2283); The Mystic Angler, 35D Williams Avenue, Mystic, CT 06355 (860-572-8633); The Fairfield Fly Shop, 917 Post Road East, Fairfield, CT 06430 (203-255-2896).

Regulatory agency: Connecticut State Fisheries, 79 Elm Street, Sixth Floor, Hartford, CT 06106 (860-424-3474), Web page http://dep.state.ct.us/.

Rhode Island

Rhode Island is a tiny state. Its shoreline, however, is nearly as long as Connecticut's. An odd piece of striper trivia is that Rhode Island is the only striper state without a large river. Fly fishing for stripers is nothing new in Rhode Island, which boasts a large club called the Rhody Fly Rodders.

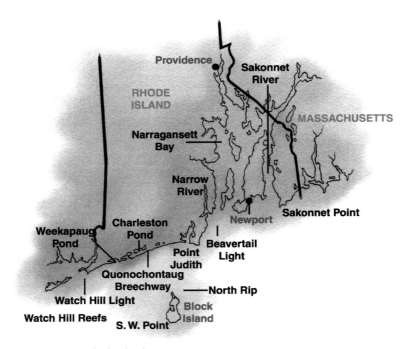

Figure 109   Rhode Island.

There are really four fishing areas in Rhode Island. First come the southern beaches. These are typical of direct ocean beaches, complete with a constant rolling swell. In back of these beaches are salt ponds, and in between are occasional rocky points of land like Watch Hill. Off Watch Hill an especially productive area called the reefs rises from the bottom and is crossed by the currents coming in and out of Long Island Sound. Moving up the coast, Weekapaug, Quonochontaug, and Charleston Breachway are shore spots that have good access. A lot of the Rhode Island southern beaches can be driven by beach buggy. Point Judith, a rocky point with great striper fishing, caps the east end of

the southern shore. The jetty that protects the west end of the Point Judith harbor of refuge, appropriately named the west wall, is regarded as one the earliest bass spots in New England: Stripers dependably appear by the middle of April, as soon as they are caught with regularity in Chesapeake Bay. The entire south-coast span is only 25 miles long, but it offers superb fishing. Every kind of bait imaginable moves along this shore and in and out of the ponds. The ponds themselves, around the first dark of the moon after mid-May, offer some of the best worm hatches on the East Coast.

Across from Point Judith lies Newport, the second fishing area. The straits between the two delineate the mouth of

Narragansett Bay; the Narragansett shore just north of Point Judith can be thought of as the approach to the bay. There is a lot of good shore fishing here, including an area of rocky shore called the avenues and perhaps the premium location, the Narrow River—really a sort of long salt pond in back of the beach. The entrance to it, on the dropping tide, has accounted for many striper blitzes. Several small rivers feed into the upper stretches of Narragansett Bay, making it a fertile residence for baitfish. In good times the bay is filled with bunker, and some record bass are taken. The Warren River, in the upper bay, is a famous producer of mostly smaller bass—but occasional cow-stripers. Immediately to the east, arguably part of Narragansett Bay, is the Sakonnet River. The shoreline of the lower Sakonnet as well as many places, such as Prudence Island, inside the bay are striper hot spots.

Third, Sakonnet Point, the nearby shoreline, Newport, and Jamestown offer headland-type rocky-beach surf casting. In Newport, Fort Adams State Park offers a brand of fly fishing from rocky ledges that has been nicknamed cliff fishing. Brenton Point State Park also offers shore fishing; a hot spot is an obvious structure called the rockpile. These areas are well known for bass of all sizes, although they are particularly famous for a big push of small fish late in the fall migration.

Finally, little Rhode Island owns one of the gems of saltwater fly fishing: Block Island. I often fished at Block Island during the 1980s, as the last generation of big stripers was dying out. In the summer there are a lot of people, and while there is sufficient public shore access, this place really shines in the fall. After Labor Day the population drops to almost zero and the large Atlantic herring move inshore. I roamed around the island at night and caught some monster fish. The 1997 season, while it didn't produce the 40- and 50-pounders of the 1980s, was an excellent year. The rocky shores of Old Harbor Point and the jetties at the mouth of a salt pond called New Harbor are two excellent fly-fishing spots. Boaters can fish Black Rock, Grove Point, Southwest Point, and the tremendous rip that forms off the north tip of the island. This is big water, and boaters should beware.

Contacts

Cove Edge Tackle, 93 Watch Hill Road, Westerly, RI 02891 (401-348-8888); The Saltwater Edge, 561 Thames Street, Newport, RI 02840 (401-842-0062), e-mail saltedge@edgenet.net, Web page http://www.saltwateredge.com; Oceans and Ponds, Inc., 217 Ocean Avenue, P.O. Box 136, Block Island, RI 02807 (401-466-5131).

Regulatory agency: Rhode Island Department of Environmental Management, 235 Promenade Street, Fourth Floor, Providence, RI 02908 (401-277-6605), Web page http://www.state.ri.us/stdept/sd27.htm.

Massachusetts

Of the northern states—and probably of all the states—Massachusetts offers the most to striper fishermen. The striper is as important to the heritage and culture of Cape Cod and the Islands as it is to Maryland's Eastern Shore. But the good fishing and interest in stripers aren't confined to this section of Massachusetts. I know the state well, and as I ponder its map, I realize that virtually every inch of the coast is good striper water.

The west shore of Buzzards Bay starts with the area around the Westport River. The mouth of the Westport, Horseneck Beach, and Gooseberry Island are great shore-fishing spots, with reasonable access. Moving east from New Bedford we come first to West Island, the one-time home of an important turn-of-the-century striper club; then to the Wareham River, an excellent estuarine fishery for stripers. Herring run up the numerous freshwater

Figure 110   Massachusetts.

inlets of this shore, providing large baits in the late spring and young-of-the-year in the fall. The Cape Cod Canal lies at the north end of Buzzards Bay and effectively makes an island of the Cape. The canal itself, with its steep banking, is difficult but not impossible to fly fish—and because of the tremendous currents that run through, it's a great striper fishery. Running off the southwest corner of the Cape are the Elizabeth Islands. Except Cuttyhunk, these islands are privately owned and must be fished from a boat. Sow and Pigs Reef, just off Cuttyhunk, has seen the capture of several world-record-class stripers. Chucking big flies into the current-scoured boulders of the Elizabeths will yield some big bass. Off the Cape's south side lie, first, the Vineyard and Nantucket Sounds, then the Islands themselves. Tides run as fast as 3 knots throughout this large area. The Cape, the Islands, and the bottoms of the sounds are made of glacial sand and gravel; they're constantly eroding and changing shape. The result is the formation of almost-infinite numbers of excellent feeding areas for stripers, available from shore and boat. Lobsterville Beach and Cape Pogue on Martha's Vineyard, as well as Smith Point and Great Point on Nantucket, are just a few of the many incredible striper spots that local fly shops can send you to.

Back on the Cape, salt ponds and inlets all along the south side provide a great supply of bait for the migrating stripers. The season starts with schoolies as early as late April here, and it lasts well into November. Sand flats extending west from 10-mile-long Monomoy Island are the scene of a summerlong sight fishery. The rip at the tip of Monomoy, as well as the numerous rips in the sounds, are productive but potentially perilous places to fish sinking lines from a boat. In the rips, the water can become so shallow that the steep waves can tumble over, easily swamping and rolling over a good-size boat.

The outside of Cape Cod is one unbroken and undeveloped stretch of open beach. The Great Beach, as it has been called by numerous romantics, is 50 miles of largely government-owned parkland. Some beach-buggy access is allowed. Among the spots most friendly to fly casters is the entrance to Pleasant Bay in Chatham, which produces huge numbers of bass annually. So do the rips, also shore accessible, at the Provincetown end of the cape. These few spots I've mentioned don't begin to do the Cape justice, however. Cape Cod Bay, Sandy Neck Beach, Scoton Creek, Nauset Inlet; the list goes on and on. It would truly be easier to list the parts of the Cape where fly fishing for stripers is of poor quality. On the other hand, I can't think of any!

Immediately across the east end of the canal from Cape Cod is Scusset State

Beach, where the beach and canal can be accessed here from a public park. At the end of the canal in this park, you can work the obvious gravel point just east of the dolphins, and have room for a backcast. Just around the corner from the canal, Scusset Beach itself is a superior spot.

Duxbury Bay is the best of a lot of great striper fishing as we head away from the Cape toward Boston. Fishing can hold late in this area, too. One September morning in the early 1980s, I tagged a 40-pound-plus striper in Maine's Kennebec River. The fish was recaptured within a day or two of Thanksgiving at White Horse Beach—just outside Duxbury Harbor and, coincidentally, Plymouth Rock. The North River is another excellent spot along this stretch, known as the South Shore.

Boston Harbor, itself the island-studded mouth of the Charles River, has tide rips, bait, shore access, and lots of stripers. Some of the islands are parks that provide access for both fishing and camping. An entire book could be written about fly-fishing opportunities for stripers in and around Boston Harbor.

The bait situation throughout all of southern Massachusetts is very diverse, and a good selection of fly sizes and colors is called for. There are herring everywhere in the spring; squid in the sound's rips; mullet in the Elizabeths; spearing, crabs, and worms in the ponds; and lots of sand eels and spearing around the Cape and Island shorelines. In the fall these are joined by baby bunker, butterfish, and herring.

The jewel of the North Shore of Massachusetts is the complex comprised of Plum Island, Cranes Beach, and the Merrimack and Ipswich rivers. The Merrimack supports large runs of shad and herring, and in late May and June, large stripers enter the river to feed on these baitfish. During the summer and into the early fall stripers are present along the beaches, where they feed on sand eels and herring. Inside the mouth of the Merrimack, the Coast Guard Beach and Joppa Flats both provide shore anglers with excellent wade- and boat-fishing possibilities. There are several ramps serving the area, including a good one right in Newburyport, near the river's mouth. Throughout the 1990s, menhaden have been scarce in New England waters. Recently, they have been practically nonexistent north of Long Island Sound. One exception has been the Plum Island–Cape Ann area, where bunker schools have provided some terrific action for big stripers. The Cape Ann shoreline is infested with ledges that provide excellent habitat for big fish. Boat fishermen do particularly well in this area by casting into the surf at the edge of the rocks. More protected-water boat fishing is available in the Essex and

Annisquam rivers; there are good ramps on each. Shore access is also good in this area since Cranes Beach and much of Plum Island are in the hands of conservation groups that allow shore fishing. The areas around Marblehead, Salem Sound, and the Beverly and Danvers rivers are also big striper producers. There are a number of rocky islands off this stretch, where anglers cast big flies on sinking lines into the turbulence near shore and catch some very respectable fish. This entire area is one of the best pieces of big-fish waters that there is. I'm certain that at least one 48-inch striper was taken by the fly in 1997, and that's the biggest I heard of anywhere!

Contacts

South Shore and Cape Cod: Fishing the Cape, Harwich Commons, Route 137, East Harwich, MA 02645 (508-432-1200); Henry Weston Outfitters, 15 Columbia Road, Pembroke, MA 02359 (617-826-7411), e-mail JIM@HWOFlyFishing.com; Coop's Bait and Tackle, R.F.D. Box 19, 147 West Tisbury Road, Edgartown, MA 02539 (508-627-8202); Cross Rip Outfitters, Nantucket Island, MA 02554 (508-228-4900), e-mail crossrip@nantucket.net.

Boston and north: Stoddard's, 50 Temple Place, Boston, MA 02111 (617-426-4187); River's Edge Trading Company, 50 Dodge Street, Beverly, MA 01915 (978-921-8008), e-mail RTrading co@aol.com.

Regulatory agency: Massachusetts Division of Marine Fisheries, 100 Cambridge Street, Boston, MA 02202 (617-727-3193), Web page http://www.state.ma.us/dfwele/dmf/dmf_toc.htm.

New Hampshire

New Hampshire has a very short coast; nonetheless it holds some excellent striper-fishing spots. Flanked by the ledgy, fishy shoreline that runs from Breaking Rock to Boars Head lies a big marshy estuary. Inside the mouth, the Blackwater River splits from the Hampton River, which is finally left by the Taylor River. If you've ever seen a big flock of gulls in late May just south of the New Hampshire tollbooths, where a small lake sits on the western side of the road and a big marsh abuts the other, you have driven over the Taylor River at alewife time. At just such a time years ago, I was headed home from Martha's Vineyard when the wheeling gulls caused me to pull over for a look. The

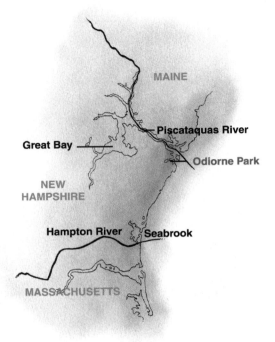

Figure 111   New Hampshire.

river, just as it went under the road, was choked with these anadromous herring. Somewhere not too far away some well-fed stripers were undoubtedly charging their own toll on the fecund alewives. All three of these rivers wind and twist for miles through tidewater grasses and mud flats. A rich bait chain exists that is very heavy in young eels, one of the striper's favorite foods. The structure in this area includes points, drop-offs, cut banks, creek mouths, and draining marshes. This is much like fishing the Chesapeake Bay's Eastern Shore, but the tides and velocity of the current flow are much greater. Stripers of all sizes are taken here, and I'm told that despite an

excellent ramp on the Seabrook shore, the Taylor River sees little pressure, especially not compared to the nearby Merrimack.

The second important water in New Hampshire is the Piscataqua River. The headwater of the Piscataqua, Great Bay, is fed by several freshwater rivers, which produces a large, tidal, freshwater bay rich in anadromous fish life. Good all-tide ramps are tough to come by on the Piscataqua; the best one is in Eliot, Maine (the lower Piscataqua is the border between New Hampshire and Maine). Fly fishers in Great Bay look for bass busting bait on the surface—more common here than elsewhere on the river. They also fish the tide lines and back eddies caused by the strong currents and the confluences of all the rivers entering the bay. Such an attraction is the upper river–Great Bay fishery that two camps of anglers have developed: one that fishes exclusively above Interstate 95 and one that fishes only the lower river and the ocean below it. I'm told that many of the devotees of each never cross the line into the other type of fishery.

The lower Piscataquas has varied types of striper habitat. The main channel runs out into a large marshy mouth and holds plenty of large fish—it's accessible by an excellent all-tide ramp at Pierce Island in Portsmouth. There are two back channels into the river, one on the Maine side, the other in New Hampshire. One angler I spoke with said he loved to fish the New Hampshire side with a canoe, and had a friend who worked it regularly in a float tube! The whole lower river system is filled with superb structure. A 10-weight rod with a 350-grain Superhead and an assortment of Groceries comprise a perfect arsenal. Yellow works well in the silty brown waters of these northern New England rivers. Herring of all sizes are the area's most important baitfish. Shore access to fishable waters in the lower river is somewhat difficult, but Odiorne Point State Park, in New Castle, is recommended by one of the local fly shops.

Contacts

American Angling Outfitters, 23 Main Street, Salem, NH 03079 (603-893-3333 or 1-800-264-5378), Web page http://www.angling.com/.

Regulatory agency: New Hampshire Fish and Game, 225 Main Street, Durham, NH 03824 (603-868-1096), Web page http://www.wildlife.state.nh.us/.

Maine

While many stripers migrate into downeast Maine and even into Canada, the area west of Penobscot Bay holds far superior fishing for stripers. Some of Maine's finest striper fishing is in York County, the southernmost part of the state. This area is a mixture of sand-beach and rock-ledge headland, divided at intervals by small and medium-size rivers. While the coast of Maine has a season-long population of anadromous and oceangoing herring, sand eels and spearing are also abundant. In the fall bass cluster around the rivers to feed on the young of the anadromous herring as they journey out to sea. The rivers—

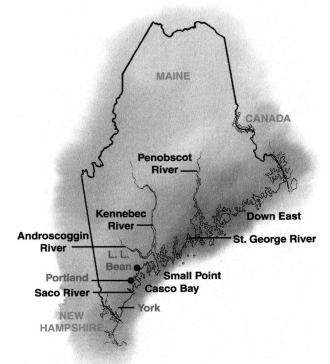

Figure 112   Maine.

York, Webhannet, Mousam, Kennebunk, and Saco, to name only a few—are great places to start. These rivers all get going in very early May, and fishing lasts into early October. The Mousam has a reputation as a particularly early producer. Public access is usually available near its mouth, and you have a choice between beach and jetty fishing. All-tide boat access is a big problem. Larger boats can come from the Piscataquas, Mousam, York, or Saco rivers, where all-tide ramps are available. There are smaller tidal ramps here and there for tin boaters or cartoppers.

Shore anglers can find riverine fishing for mostly schoolie stripers inside many of the rivers. The York, Mousam, and Saco are particularly good. Shore access is limited, so check with the contacts listed here. York, Wells, Drakes Island, Ogunquit, and Old Orchard beaches have good surf fishing. One of the area's great fly fishers told me that a pollack-colored Groceries (white belly, olive green top) is the top fly.

Around the greater Portland area the Scarboro Marsh complex, Spurwink River, and Presumpscot River are known producers. The area has plenty of boat access, but it can be tough at dead-low tide.

Heading north, the islands of Casco Bay and the passages between them all hold bass in the central part of the summer. You need a midsize boat to work this area.

After Casco Bay you enter the midcoast of Maine. Sand beaches (with the exception of the area around the Kennebec's mouth) now become quite rare, and the shoreline gets deep closer to shore than it does in York County. This also means that the water is typically cooler, shortening the season by at least a couple of weeks on each end. The New Meadows, Kennebec, Sheepscot, Damariscotta, Medomak, and Saint George rivers all come from freshwater sources to separate long rocky headlands that jut well out into the Gulf of Maine. Each of these rivers supports runs of anadromous herring, eels, smelts, and tomcod; in the summer their lower reaches are packed with grass shrimp, and serve as the nursery ground for vast shoals of young Atlantic herring as well. The rivers themselves are filled and emptied by 10-foot tides that create incredible currents. All of them have excellent fishing for bass of all sizes.

The Kennebec, however, is in a class with few peers. One of Maine's favorite sons, Robert Tristram Coffin, once wrote about the Kennebec, the shores of which were home to his family: "Doubtless the Lord could have made a better river for fish than the Kennebec. . . . But he never did." The Kennebec runs some 10 miles to Bath, where it starts

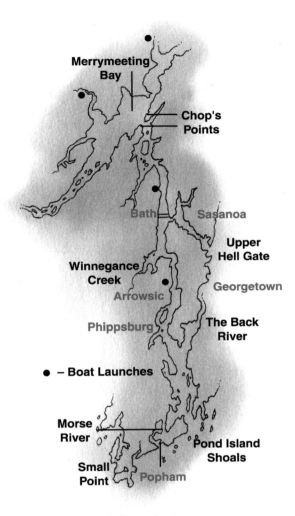

Figure 113   Detail of Kennebec River.

becoming brackish, then a like distance to reach totally fresh Merrymeeting Bay. This bay is a large tidal lake fed by five freshwater rivers, plus the Kennebec itself. The river is the only known American striped bass spawning site north of the Hudson, and the only site of a successful striper reintroduction. In a cooperative program between the state and private individuals, Hudson River and probably Chesapeake Bay fingerlings were stocked into the river during the 1980s. Within a very few years young-of-the-year stripers started to show up in stream surveys, and have ever since. Stripers of all sizes like the Kennebec. The lower reaches of the river have produced many 40- and 50-pound stripers, and even a few of over 60 pounds. In the 1890s a 90-pound striper was taken through the ice at Bath, Maine.

There is a reasonable amount of shore access all through midcoast Maine: This is still a lightly developed part of the world. The foot of the dam on the Kennebec in Augusta and the reversing falls on the Sheepscot both provide shore fishing for schoolies by mid-May. Popham Beach State Park provides excellent beach fly fishing for stripers, especially at the mouth of the Morse River. For boat fishermen, there are good launching facilities on all of these rivers, particularly the Kennebec.

At this point we are near the end of the striper's abundant range, and the bass are largely gone from this part of Maine by the end of September. No problem, though: They're still in the Merrimack, and in late October things will be getting hot south of Cape Cod. Montauk peaks in November, and the bass are already schooling on the Jersey Shore, down the Delmarva Peninsula, and off the bay bridge tunnel. In December the last roundup starts down at Cape Point and continues until early January.

That's about the time of year it is now, as I write the last of this book—and when I'm finished I'll start tying flies, refurbishing tackle, and generally making serious plans for the 1998 season. Writing and researching this book have certainly given me a few new ideas. The old saying should perhaps be changed to "So many stripers, so little time!" Brock Apfel's fishing widow, Joan, once growled at him that his love of striper fishing was an affliction; one, he replied, that she would be fortunate to have.

Contacts

Maine coast: L.L. Bean Retail Store, Route 1, Freeport, ME 04033-0001 (1-800-347-4552), Web page http://www.llbean.com/; Eldredge Bros. Fly Shop, Route 1, Cape Neddick, ME 03902 (207-363-2004), Web page http://www.eldredgeFlyShop.com; Spar Cove Outfitters, 260 Commercial St., Portland, ME 04101 (207-772-4222).

Regulatory agency: Maine Department of Marine Resources, 21 State House Station, Augusta, ME 04333 (207-624-6550), Web page http://www.state.me.us/dep/mdephome.htm.

SAVING STRIPERS

A few years ago I told a friend that it was a great time to be alive, if you were a striped bass fisherman. I'd hold to that statement, especially with several great year-classes of stripers about to enter the coastal fishery. All is, however, not as rosy as proclaimed by the Atlantic States Marine Fisheries Commission—the organization of state fisheries managers currently in charge of striped bass regulations. At this writing, the Chesapeake Bay commercial striper fishery has been completely restored to its long-term average catch rate. Meanwhile, coastal anglers are still patiently conserving stripers by releasing well over 90 percent of their catch. In my travels I have found that anglers all along the coast share the same observations and concerns. Each spring a fresh group of mostly three-year-old, 16-inch stripers leave their nursery grounds for the first time and move northward along the coast. Since they are too small for legal possession in all jurisdictions, they are still very abundant. These fish return each fall as 18- to 20-inch stripers, which can legally be captured by the mid-Atlantic commercial fishery. The coastal anglers wait for the next year, expecting to see these same fish return as schools of low-20-inch stripers—but they don't. The depletion in their numbers is simply amazing. In a more conservatively managed fishery these fish would indeed come back, and would join smaller but still abundant numbers of mid-20-inch fish, and so on upward in size until we reached a much smaller, but still obvious number of 40- and 50-pound individuals.

Despite (or perhaps because of) a numbingly complex assortment of fisheries statistics and mathematical population projections that predict solid year-class distribution, it isn't happening. It is not happening with stripers, and it is not happening in any coastal fishery today. This is not to say that there aren't any larger stripers, because there are, but they don't approach the numbers that should exist.

Additionally, the recreational fishing public is being effectively prohibited—by assigning minimum sizes and/or season closures—from catching its own fish. These fish are then allocated to commercial fishermen. The current 28-inch minimum size along the coast means that many anglers, especially those who cannot afford a boat, will fail to catch even one legal fish in an entire season! Even the Chesapeake Bay's recreational anglers, who can keep two small bass per day, can only do so for three months. The commercial season in the bay, however, lasts for nine months. Even given the constraints of this very modest daily bag limit, recreational anglers could easily harvest all of the stripers that ought to be removed annually from the population—and more.

When freshwater fish, wild bird, and game animal populations reached this point, commercial harvest was prohibited. Why not stripers? Yes, this would cut off the nonfishing public's supply of wild striped bass. But there are 10 times as many people in this country as there are stripers; some allocation process is necessary. The precedent with other scarce resources has been to give at least a modest daily bag limit to individual citizens willing to go to the effort to catch their own. That, unfortunately, is all the striped bass that are available. I see no one complaining today because they can't buy wild black ducks or brook trout in the supermarket. Giving the striper protection throughout its range as a gamefish or personal-use species would allow for the quality management of the fishery and add dramatically to its economic and social value to the citizenry. It would also provide the striped bass aquaculture industry, which already grows more pounds of striper fillets than are generated by the wild popula-

Figure 114   Father and son with a pair of stripers. This size made up the majority of the fishing in 1996 and 1997.

tion, an incentive to replace the wild fish in the markets. Atlantic salmon aquaculture has shown us what can happen: More people would ultimately be able to enjoy a meal of striped bass than can do so today. In addition to all of this it's well known that every striper caught commercially has only a tiny portion of the economic value it would have had if harvested recreationally, or allowed to live and grow to the size that drives hordes of recreational anglers to feverishly pursue it. Commercial striper fishing, per-haps once a worthwhile industry, is today a kind of societal self-deprivation.

The Coastal Conservation Association, which has eliminated inshore gillnetting and made the redfish a personal-use species (or gamefish) throughout most of the South, now is resolved to see the striped bass protected nationally as a gamefish. This organization is the saltwater sport fishermen's best voice, both state by state and nationally. There are CCA chapters in nearly all the states of the striper's range, and many have their own Web pages. Become a member, choose the level of activity you're comfortable with, but whatever you do, add your number to our ranks. A large and organized membership is the key to receiving due consideration in future man-agement decisions.

All of this is not to say that as recreational fishers we are doing everything we should for conservation. Whether we fish with live bait, conventional tackle, or flies, we can all do more to eliminate unwanted mortality. Use tackle heavy enough to quickly subdue stripers. There is no virtue in whipping a fish to near death by using scrawny leaders and ultralightweight rods. Stripers should be brought to hand long before they lose their ability to stay upright in the water.

Figure 115   Hooked in the lip, brought to hand, and released in a well-oxygenated quiet spot—this striper will recover. (Photo by Pip Winslow)

Figure 116   *Circle hooks.* (Courtesy *Field & Stream*)

Don't remove the fish from the water unless necessary. If you want a photograph, prepare your equipment before you remove the fish from the water. Be careful to support the fish's belly and spine, and *return the fish to the water quickly.*

Have a hook disgorger and/or a pair of long-nose pliers handy. Use them, if necessary, while the fish is still in the water. It is amazing how the slightest twist of a pair of pliers can accomplish more than a strong man's greatest efforts with his fingertips.

Avoid flies that bass will swallow. Soft, tiny flies and poppers are frequently inhaled by stripers. I know that anglers love to see bass take poppers from the surface—but they kill a lot of fish. Since stripers cannot see the popper clearly in the surface film, they charge it with their mouth wide open, swallowing everything they can get their lips around. The popper's hook often ends up back in the gills. And on top of this hooking damage, the popper body also obscures its shank, making the fly tough to remove. I have

Figure 117   *Stripping gloves also keep hands from being abraided by the striper's rough mouth. Note hook in corner of the mouth.* (Photo by Duncan Barnes)

Figure 118a   Bending a finished fly's hook.

Before

After

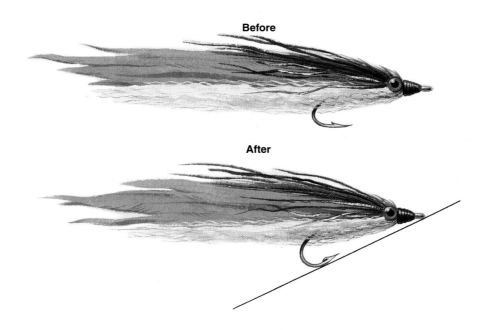

Figure 118b   Before and After

stopped using poppers except as occasional search instruments, or on shallow, still-water fish that simply won't hit a fly they can see well. Usually a spun-hair slider will catch just as many of these fussy fish, and without the deep-hooking problems.

Several years ago I started copying the circle hook intended for use on commercial long lines by bending my fly hooks as shown in the illustration. I found a tremendous increase in the number of fish that I hooked in the lips, rather than the inside of the mouth or the gills. By continuing the bend inward, the hook can slide along without catching until it exits the mouth. The edge created by the lips then enters the hook gap, and the point bites in. While not infallible, it does eliminate most internal hooking. A significant additional benefit is that the circular nature of the hook, coupled with the tough, fibrous nature of the lip, assures that a higher percentage of the stripers that are hooked will be landed. This is especially true of larger bass, which are commonly hooked by the soft skin inside of their mouths; later in the fight, though, the skin breaks and the hook pulls free. I've tested this hook on thousands of stripers, and the professionals at *Field & Stream* magazine have tested it as well. This **conservation bend** works not only on stripers but also on other large-mouthed swallowers of prey.

Hooks should be bent before you begin, since some breakage will occur in the bending process. You can, however, bend the hooks on finished flies that you already have. I have broken a few hooks while bending them, though I have never broken one on a fish.

I am more confident when I fish for stripers with flies that have the conservation bend. And I love knowing that I am exacting a very low level of hooking mortality on the stripers I release.

INDEX